Portrait of a Decade

The 1930s

CHARLES FREEMAN

B.T. Batsford Ltd, London

Contents

The original idea for the Portrait of a Decade series was conceived by Trevor Fisher.

Typeset by Tek-Art Ltd Kent
and printed and bound
in Great Britain by
MacLehose and Partners Ltd, Portsmouth
for the publishers
B.T. Batsford Ltd
4 Fitzhardinge Street
London W1H 0AH

A CIP catalogue record for this book is available from the British Library

ISBN 0 7134 6073 3

Frontispiece: The 'Jarrow Crusade' of 1936: 200 unemployed men walked the 300 miles from Jarrow in the North East to London, to ask for the Government's help in providing jobs for the town.

Introduction

The last years of the 1920s had been years of hope. Memories of the horrors of the First World War were at last fading, and for many it seemed that war was a thing of the past. The world economy was prosperous too, that is until the Wall Street Crash in 1929. In the USA thousands were ruined, and the money they had lent overseas had to be hurriedly called back home, destroying the overseas businesses which had relied on it. In order to protect its own industry and farmers, the USA then passed tariff laws which prevented foreign goods coming into the country. Other nations followed its example and this led to a slump in world trade as each nation shut itself off from others. A world depression was under way.

First and foremost the Depression meant misery for millions who had lost their jobs. By 1932 there were 6 million unemployed in Germany, 3 million in Britain and over 12 million in the USA. In Japan millions of peasants were ruined as happened in other countries which depended on the export of food and raw materials for their income. Unemployment hit not only workers and small farmers. The middle classes were equally affected as small businesses and even banks collapsed. Few governments seemed able to cope with the crisis.

To many it seemed that only the energy and authority of a strong leader could offer the chance for a nation to fight its way out of the Depression, which was one reason why the 1930s became an age of dictators. Some dictators had become established in the 1920s. In 1922 Benito Mussolini had set up the world's first Fascist state in Italy. Fascism glorified the nation, praising strong leadership and military strength. In the Soviet Union Lenin had established a very different type of dictatorship, one based on the needs of one class, the workers. Lenin's Communist state, the first in the world, developed into a more brutal form of dictatorship under his successor, Josef Stalin, who was firmly in power by 1929 and determined to transform the Soviet Union into an industrial giant.

As the Depression scarred Germany, millions rallied to the call of the Nazi Party, led by Adolf Hitler. German Nazism had many similarities with Italian Fascism. It too glorified the nation, the race and military strength. Hitler came to power in 1933 and was to use his power more brutally and efficiently than Mussolini ever did. Another military state was Japan where the army, filled with recruits from ruined peasant families, was already expanding overseas, taking over the Chinese province of Manchuria in 1931.

Dictators, whether Fascist, Nazi or Communist, seemed attractive to many at a time of economic despair. The dictators promised action and the restoration of pride. In the Soviet Union the Five Year Plans, massive plans to expand industry, seemed particularly successful when compared to the industrial decay in the Western capitalist nations. In Germany by 1936 unemployment had fallen to 1 million from 6 million four years earlier.

What many failed to see, or perhaps chose not to see, was the brutal suppression of human rights in these dictatorships, a suppression hidden effectively behind the propaganda which helped keep the dictators in power. Propaganda and terror used together were effective instruments of control. At the same time the policies of Hitler, Mussolini and the Japanese leaders all contained threats of aggression against their neighbours.

Some nations remained firmly attached to democracy. Perhaps the most successful was the USA where Franklin Roosevelt, elected first in 1932, and

The Empire State Building, New York, was a triumph of 1930s construction and remained the tallest structure in the world until 1954.

3

Introduction

During the Depression many of the unemployed in the USA were reduced to living in shanty homes. Despite everything, the American flag still flies.

then again in 1936 by a massive majority, brought inspiration and some recovery to a nation shattered by the Depression. Britain, too, maintained its democratic ideals in the 1930s, although its governments were hardly ones which inspired the people. Other democracies were less stable. France was increasingly weakened by its political squabbling, just at a time when it needed to stand firm against the rising power of Nazi Germany. In Spain democracy collapsed in 1936 when the country became split by a bitter and brutal civil war.

The democracies saw slow but steady economic recovery after 1932, and their peoples were able to take advantage of the new inventions of the age. Radio spread to most homes by the end of the decade. In Britain television was coming in for a few lucky viewers. For the first time the middle-class family could enjoy its own car and some electrical goods, such as vacuum cleaners and fridges. These were not major changes but they brought back some hope and stability after the turmoil of the early 1930s.

Every age has its heroes, and in the 1930s these were often aviators, such as Amy Johnson and Amelia Earhart, or land speed champions like Sir Malcolm Campbell. The cinema was also extraordinarily popular. The great Hollywood studios produced the extravagant musicals of Busby Berkeley, Fred Astaire and Ginger Rogers in their dance routines, and child stars such as Shirley Temple and Judy Garland. Other favourite themes were horror movies, gangster films and, from 1939, westerns.

All these attractions took people's minds off the real issues of the age. The greatest failure of the democracies was in foreign affairs, for by the middle of the 1930s it had become clear that war was no longer a thing of the past.

The first ominous sign that peace might not last had come as early as 1931 when the Japanese army took control of the Chinese province of Manchuria. In 1935, the Italian dictator, Mussolini, aware that his regime was losing support, decided to revive its fortunes by attacking the weak independent state of Abyssinia (now Ethiopia) in East Africa. Nothing effective was done to stop him, and with the help of poison gas he emerged as the victor. In 1936 a conflict of a very different kind broke out in Spain when the country was rent by a bitter civil war. The war, with its terror and bombings of civilian towns, had a massive impact on the world, and thousands of outsiders came to fight on either side. In 1937 the Japanese were on the move again, launching an attack southwards into China and using mass bombing to conquer the coastal towns. By this time no one could argue that the use of violence between and within nations was a thing of the past.

While the USA, cut off from the world by two major oceans, could, and did, turn its back on such events, Britain and France could not. Both had empires in the Far East which could easily be threatened by Japan and there seemed very little they could do to defend them. Neither had been able or willing to spend much on defence and their weakness became all too clear when Germany started to rearm.

France was the most threatened. It was surrounded by Spain to the south, Germany to the north and Italy to the south-east. There was always the fear that Germany might seek revenge on France after its defeat in the First World War. From 1936 Italy was drawing closer to Germany, leaving France isolated. Internally, France was economically weak and politically unstable. Its foreign policy in these years became increasingly paralysed.

Shirley Temple, here seen in Stand Up and Cheer!, *was one of the film stars who helped cheer up the world during the 1930s.*

Introduction

As a result France followed the lead of Britain, and from 1937 Britain had at last a leader who was determined to bring peace to a troubled Europe. Neville Chamberlain, the new Prime Minister, believed it was not only possible but vital to make a deal with Adolf Hitler of Germany. Chamberlain knew that Britain, alone or with only a weak France for support, could hardly fight both Japan and Germany together.

In 1938 Hitler moved into Austria. He then turned his attention to the German-speaking peoples of Czechoslovakia, claiming that they were being persecuted by the Czechs. Their lands, he claimed, should be joined to Germany.

In September 1938 Chamberlain made no less than three visits to Germany to try to settle the dispute between Germany and Czechoslovakia. At the third visit, to Munich, Chamberlain, with French support, agreed that Hitler *could* take over the Sudeten area of Czechoslovakia where the Germans lived. This proved to be a fatal mistake. Hitler became convinced Britain and France would always give in to him and, furthermore, he was now in a strong position to move further into Czechoslovakia and the rest of Eastern Europe.

The odd one out in all this was the Soviet Union. Stalin knew that Germany was his major threat. He had hoped that Britain and France might join him in an alliance against the Germans. However, increasingly he lost faith in their strength and willingness to stand up to Hitler. Britain and France had their own suspicions of Stalin and so no deal was ever made.

In August 1939 Stalin made an extraordinary move. He signed an agreement with Germany under which both nations agreed not to attack each other. This is all the world was told. Secretly, they also agreed to carve up the state of Poland between them. Stalin knew he would probably end up fighting Germany in the end, but in the short term it was worth buying time in which to build up his defences.

On 1 September Hitler attacked Poland. Although France and Britain did eventually declare war against him, there was, by now, nothing they could do to save the Poles. Poland was crushed within a few weeks of fighting and found itself occupied by both Germany and the Soviet Union. The Second World War was under way.

If the Second World War had not come, we might have judged the 1930s as a moderately successful decade in world history. It was an age when conditions slowly improved for many people, when advances in medicine and scientific knowledge were gradually making life better. The Depression *was* conquered eventually.

However, the outbreak of war, particularly one in which the mass extermination of Jews and other civilians took place in gas chambers, labour camps and by bombers, has condemned the 1930s as a decade of failure. Certainly, the governments of the democracies, Britain, France and the USA in particular, were unable, for a variety of reasons, to deal creatively with the problems of foreign policy. They seldom had the imagination to realize just how serious were the threats posed by the dictators, not only to human rights but to the hopes that nations could live in peace. Fifty years on, our own world is still recovering from the war the dictators caused, but which the democracies were unable to prevent. To that extent this was a decade of failure. It remains one, however, with many lessons to teach us.

George VI and his family wave to the crowds from Buckingham Palace after his coronation in 1937. Despite the abdication of Edward VIII, the monarchy continued to enjoy enormous respect throughout the decade.

1930 Collective farms:

Collective farms forced on to peasants

MILLIONS OF PEASANTS, who since the Revolution of 1917 had been allowed to keep and farm their own plots of land, were driven into collective farms under the new policy of Stalin's government. It is estimated that half of the country's 25 million peasants were in the farms by March 1930. They had been promised that the new farms would have electric power and tractors, but in most cases these had not been provided.

There were reports of widespread opposition from peasants who were slaughtering their animals and destroying their tools, rather than bringing them into the farms. In some areas they were forced in at gunpoint.

The hope of the government was that the new farms would help solve Russia's food shortages. More food was desperately needed for the millions of workers moving into the new cities created by the Five Year Plans, which aimed to transform Russia into a major industrial state. The government claimed that the new collective farms, backed by modern farming techniques, would be much more efficient than the small and backward peasant farms.

The policy was enforced most strongly in the richer grain-growing areas of the Soviet Union such as the Ukraine and the Volga region as these offered the best hopes for increased production.

Tough new kulak policy

THE MOST BRUTAL part of the collectivization programme was the government's treatment of the kulaks, the richer peasants. In a decree of 4 February it was announced that this class was an enemy of the state and, in Stalin's words, 'must be smashed in open battle'. Kulaks were divided into three groups. Firstly, 'any organizers and perpetrators of terrorist acts' were to be isolated and sent to concentration camps. Secondly, kulaks who showed 'the slightest active resistance' were to

chaos in Russia

be deported to remote areas of the country and put to work cutting down forests or labouring on farms. The rest were not to be allowed to join the collective farms but were to be given poorer land alongside them.

The kulaks, with their families an estimated 6 million people, could hardly be called rich by the standards of the rest of Europe, but the Soviet government, and Stalin in particular, saw them as a major threat to the government's plans to take total control of the economy. Hundreds of thousands of kulaks disappeared into labour camps or exile in the months that followed.

Class war in the villages

THE CLASS WAR in the villages becomes more ruthless daily. A decree promulgated today by the Council of People's Commissars empowers local executives to oust and exile the kulaks . . . the kulaks' entire possessions – house, stock and implements – will be handed over to the nearest collective farm. These 'gifts' to collectives are to be regarded as contributions made by the village poor who thus are stimulated to hate the kulaks. *New York Times*, reporting from Moscow in February 1930.

Josef Stalin was absolute ruler of the Soviet Union and responsible for its transformation into an industrial state.

Stalin relaxes the programme

BY MARCH 1930 Stalin realized his government's programme was going desperately wrong. The sowing season would soon be under way but the old farms had been destroyed and the new ones not yet operating. Unless order was restored, Russia faced economic disaster. In an article in the Communist Party newspaper, *Pravda*, called 'Dizzy with Success', Stalin announced that the programme must be slowed down. He blamed local officials for pushing collectivization too fast. At once the collective farms collapsed as peasants hurried back to their original plots. In the central Black Earth areas of Russia three-quarters of the collective farms ceased to operate. Stalin was to renew the collectivization programme later in the year.

Five Year Plan under way

THE FIRST FIVE YEAR PLAN, aimed at transforming the Soviet Union from an agricultural to an industrial economy, was by now well under way. It had a target of tripling the production of coal, iron, steel, oil and machinery. Electrical power was to increase by 600 per cent. Vast new industrial plants were being built, including ironworks at Magnitogorsk beyond the Ural mountains, a great industrial area in the Donetz Basin in the Ukraine and oil wells in the Caucasus. It was the most ambitious plan the world had ever seen.

World News

World Depression under way?

FOLLOWING THE DRAMATIC COLLAPSE of the American stock market in October 1929, there were increasing signs of a major economic depression spreading through the world. By March 1930 unemployment in the USA was up to 3,250,000. In an attempt to protect American industry, tariffs were placed on foreign goods coming to America. This meant that many other nations lost one of their best markets and their economies began to suffer. Many, including Australia, France, India, Italy, Mexico, Spain and Switzerland, put up their tariffs too, cutting international trade still further. Prices fell throughout the world and so did profits.

Monthly value of world trade in US dollars: January 1930 2,739 million; December 1,839 million.

The unemployment queues lengthen. Here a soup kitchen in Chicago, USA, provides for the poor.

Nazis increase their support

IN GERMANY THINGS became particularly desperate as US investors withdrew the money they had lent to the country, and there too unemployment was soon up to 3 million. In elections held in September, the National Socialist (Nazi) Party, led by Adolf Hitler, achieved a major success by increasing its number of votes from 809,000 in 1928 to 6,400,000 and, with

107 seats, became the second largest party in the Reichstag, the German parliament.

Hitler drew a great deal of his new support from the middle classes, who were increasingly anxious about the effects of the Depression, and from farmers in the northern parts of Germany who were suffering from falling prices for their produce. At the same time he attracted the young unemployed. Two-thirds of the Nazi stormtroopers (the SA) in Berlin and Hamburg were unemployed, and they found strength and meaning in joining the ranks of a party which promised action and renewal for Germany.

Gandhi's salt march

ONCE AGAIN THE INDIAN nationalist leader Mahatma Gandhi embarrassed the British government in India with a campaign against the salt tax. All salt in India was subject to tax which fell most heavily on the poorest Indians.

Gandhi decided to lead a protest march of 300 miles through India to the coast, where he would pick up a piece of salt from the shore. Although Gandhi was now 61, he completed the

The British King, George V, addresses the delegates at the London Naval Conference.

march in 24 days, arousing tremendous enthusiasm in every village he passed through. He arrived at the coast at Dandi on 5 April and on 6 April collected a piece of salt left by the sea.

His peaceful action brought turmoil. As thousands followed Gandhi's example, the police moved in to make mass arrests. Over 60,000 were put in prison, including Gandhi himself. In May, police brutally beat up a group of protesters who were trying to take over some salt pans (where salt was dried), injuring some 320 of them.

Rabindranath Tagore, India's great novelist, felt these events marked the end of British prestige in India.

Those who live in India far away from the east have got to realize that Europe has completely lost her former moral prestige in Asia. She is no longer regarded as the champion throughout the world of fair dealing and the exponent of high principle, but as the upholder of Western race supremacy and the exploiter of those outside her own borders.

Naval powers make treaty

THE FIVE GREAT NAVAL POWERS, the USA, Britain, France, Japan and Italy, met in London between January and April to discuss naval disarmament. They agreed on ways of regulating submarine warfare and for a five-year ban on the construction of major new ships. Aircraft-carriers were also to be limited. The USA and Britain agreed that they would have equal tonnage of battleships, while Japan agreed to have no more than 70 per cent of the British and US tonnages. The London Naval Treaty was signed on 21 April, but France and Italy refused to accept all its provisions. The treaty was a sign of the general lack of international tension between the world's major powers in 1930.

France starts to build Maginot Line

THE LESSON OF THE FIRST WORLD WAR seemed to be that a strong line of defence was all that was needed to fight off enemies. So France decided to build a massive concrete wall along her border with Germany. Called the Maginot Line after André Maginot, the Minister for War, it was the most modern system of defence in the world. Its concrete was thicker than any known elsewhere, and inside the underground tunnels, where the soldiers were based, it was to be air-conditioned. There were to be recreation areas and living quarters underground as well as railways which could bring in reinforcements quickly. The line was expected to take several years to build and to consume a large proportion of the French defence budget.

Sport and the Arts

D.H. Lawrence dies

D.H. LAWRENCE, the controversial novelist and poet, author of *Women in Love* and *Lady Chatterley's Lover*, died of tuberculosis in France in March. Another death was that of Arthur Conan Doyle, the creator of Sherlock Holmes.

Architecture old and new

IN AN INTERNATIONAL EXHIBITION in Stockholm, Sweden, the world saw architects' visions of a new way of living. The modernists did not have it all their own way, however: in New Delhi, in India, a vast new city was being completed to reflect the grandeur of British rule in India. The Viceroy's House, the last great building to be completed, covered an area the size of the French Palace of Versailles.

Bobby Jones completes the Grand Slam

BOBBY JONES, the American golfer, achieved a Grand Slam, winning the British and American Open Titles and the British and American Amateur Titles, the first time this had ever been done. Jones' achievement was all the more remarkable because he never became a professional and was, in fact, a lawyer in his working life.

The first World Cup

THE WORLD CUP was held for the first time in 1930. However, because of disputes over where the competition should be held, many nations, including England and almost all the European footballing nations, stayed away. In the end Uruguay, the host nation, beat Argentina in the final 4-2.

Sound well-established

FILM-GOING WAS THE MOST POPULAR pastime of all in the early 1930s both in the USA and Europe. In the USA attendances ran at 110 million a week. By 1930 sound was an established part of the cinema but many actors fell from favour as soon as their voices were heard for the first time.

A major success of 1930 was *All Quiet on the Western Front*, a study of a group of German teenagers who enlist to serve in the First World War. Their enthusiasm for fighting disappears as they reach the trenches and discover the true horror of the war in which they all are killed. *All Quiet* helped develop a strong anti-war feeling among the general public, but it was banned in both Germany and Austria after protests there.

A new favourite of 1930 was Marlene Dietrich who starred in the film *The Blue Angel*. Dietrich plays a night club singer who fatally attracts and marries a middle-aged professor. He soon bores her to tears, and she humiliates him until he commits suicide.

Donald Bradman smashes English bowling

IN THE THIRD TEST between Australia and England at Leeds, Australia's Donald Bradman achieved a record score for one batsman of 334 runs, 309 of which were scored in one day, another record. This was Bradman's first visit to England. As a boy he had perfected his batting style by hitting a soft ball against a corrugated metal water tank.

R101 crashes in France

IN 1930 THERE WAS STILL GREAT FAITH in the future of the airship, and in Britain two great airships were being built, the R100, designed by Barnes Wallis and privately built and the R101, built with public money.

The prospectus for the R100 claimed that the vehicle could 'bring India within four days of England, Canada within three, Australia within eight . . . Over long distances the airship is safer, more economical and more comfortable than the aeroplane'.

In July the R100 went to Canada and back from Britain. The outward journey took 78 hours and the return journey 57 hours.

However, disaster struck the R101 in October. Setting out on a trip to India, it crashed over France with the loss of 44 lives. It seems that, soaked by heavy rain, the airship became impossible to steer properly and hit a hillside exploding on impact.

The *Blattnerphone* helps sound recording

UNTIL 1930 THE BBC experienced great problems in recording its programmes for future use, and they had to go out 'live'. However, that year a new machine, the *Blattnerphone*, was installed in BBC Headquarters in London allowing programmes to be recorded for later transmission. The Blattnerphone used steel tape six millimetres wide. This had to be cut with shears and soldered together when a programme was edited. As there was only one Blattnerphone and it was too big to be moved, all recorded programmes had to be made in the London studio.

Amy Johnson flies to Australia

THE IMAGINATION OF THE WORLD was captured by Amy Johnson, the 27-year-old daughter of a fish merchant in Hull, who flew solo from England to Australia, becoming the first woman to do this. She set out from Croydon Airport in a second-hand plane, flying for 12 hours at a stretch with little more than a packet of sandwiches and a thermos flask to keep her going. She made her way across the world to increasing enthusiasm and publicity, arriving to a huge welcome at Darwin in Northern Australia on 24 April.

Amy Johnson captured the imagination of the world by her solo flight from Britain to Australia.

Discovery of Pluto

AN AMERICAN ASTRONOMER, Clyde Tombaugh, discovered the ninth planet of the solar system this year. It was named Pluto after the Greek god of the underworld. Pluto is about the same size as the moon and is the furthest of the planets from the sun. A ninth planet had been predicted by scientists, but Tombaugh had to compare thousands of photographs of one part of the sky before he could detect the slow-moving planet.

First in 1930

A young British inventor, Frank Whittle, patented ideas for the first jet engine for aircraft.

The British Post Office started its telephone service to Australia.

Scientists in the American Du Pont company developed a new artificial fibre later known as nylon.

1931

Japanese in

Hopes for peace shattered

AT THE END OF THE 1920S there had been great hopes that the nations of the world were learning to live in peace. In 1928 many nations had signed the Kellogg-Briand Pact, an agreement that they would not use war as an instrument of policy. The League of Nations, set up after the First World War, had provided a means for nations with disputes to solve them through discussion.

However, in October, Japanese troops stationed in the large and important Chinese province of Manchuria attacked the Chinese and quickly overran the province. This was the first act of international aggression for some years and shattered the hopes that war had become a thing of the past.

Railway explosion starts attack

THE JAPANESE ATTACK on Manchuria began on 18 September with an explosion on the main railway line through the province near the large town of Mukden. The line was being guarded by Japanese troops who were protecting the supply of goods coming along this line. The Japanese announced that the attack had been launched by the Chinese and that they had immediately counter-attacked, shelling the Chinese garrison in Mukden. However, it was soon clear that the Chinese had not been involved and could do little to resist the well-organized Japanese takeover. Soon the whole of Manchuria had come under Japanese control.

Manchuria – remote but rich

MANCHURIA WAS ONE of the richest areas of China, but in the 1920s the Chinese government had very little control over the province which was ruled by local warlords. As a result China's neighbour, Japan, had forced its way in and managed to gain 'concessions', agreements allowing it to take out raw materials such as coal and iron ore via the railways to the coast.

A new Chinese government, under Chiang Kaishek, had come to power in 1928 and was determined to regain control of Manchuria. It had already gained the support of the local Chinese leaders. The Japanese army knew it must act quickly if it was to seize the province before Chiang strengthened his grip.

The urge to expand

JAPAN HAD SUFFERED particularly badly in the Depression. The exports of its main raw material, silk, had fallen by 50 per cent bringing ruin to many peasant families. These families were the traditional recruiting grounds for the army, and by 1930 their bitterness was making itself felt among the younger army officers. The best way out, they felt, was to expand on the mainland, seizing control of raw materials, and building a Japanese overseas empire. So followed the attack on Manchuria.

The Japanese government opposed the attack but proved unable to stop it. The army had clearly built itself up into a position of strength. In 1928 the army had been behind the assassination of the warlord ruler of Manchuria but those responsible had never been punished. Emperor Hirohito, who had come to the throne in 1926, did not intervene to stop the army either. The army's success in Manchuria brought it greater prestige and it now had the strength and popularity to dominate political life.

A challenge for the League

JAPAN WAS AN IMPORTANT MEMBER of the League of Nations, one of the four permanent members of its Council (the others were Britain, France and Italy). Its record in the 1920s had been good. Its act of aggression in Manchuria was, therefore, a great embarrassment for the League. Even though the Japanese government did not approve of the attack, it remained responsible for the actions of its troops.

What was to be done? China appealed to the League for help but the League moved slowly, hoping the situation could be settled by some kind of agreement between China and Japan. Meanwhile the Japanese army steadily strengthened its control of Manchuria. The Japanese government proposed that a commission should visit Manchuria to study what had happened. Eventually, in December, the commission, headed by the British Lord Lytton, was set up. It set off by boat far too late to change what had happened. Besides, the League had little power to influence events unless its other leading members were ready

Manchuria

to give it full support.

The USA was not a member. Britain and France were reluctant to do much at a time of economic depression. It was difficult to see whether Japan could be driven out from an area it now controlled. Should Japan have been condemned more strongly and trading

and other links with it cut? This may simply have driven the Japanese to further acts of aggression against China which no one in Europe would have been able to prevent.

Whatever the possible outcome of measures the League could have taken, its failure to successfully oppose the

Japanese troops in China: starting with the occupation of Manchuria in 1931, the Japanese gradually extended their control over Northern China in the 1930s.

Japanese takeover of Manchuria was a major setback for the cause of world peace.

World News

An unlikely meeting: two major but very different figures of the 1930s meet. Charlie Chaplin, the film star, was introduced to the Indian nationalist leader, Gandhi, when the latter was visiting London in 1931.

Gandhi at Round Table Conference

THE INDIAN NATIONALIST LEADER Mahatma Gandhi visited Britain in September to attend the Round Table Conference on the future of India. He continued to wear little more than a loincloth, even when visiting King George V at Buckingham Palace. During his time in Britain Gandhi lodged in the East End of London, saying he preferred to be among poor people.

The conference achieved little. The British wanted to preserve special privileges for the Indian princes whose states made up about a third of the country. Many Indian religious groups, including the Hindus, Moslems and Sikhs, insisted on having separate seats in future parliaments so that they would not be dominated by other groups. Gandhi argued that Indians had to forget their differences and act together if they were to achieve independence. He called for India to have immediate control over its own defence and foreign policy. Gandhi failed to persuade the different Indian groups to work together, and the conference broke up with little agreement on the future form of India.

Depression bites deeper

THE ECONOMIC DEPRESSION became steadily worse in 1931. Germany and Austria were among the hardest hit. The largest Austrian bank, the Credit-Anstalt, failed in May followed by one of the most important German banks, the Darmstädter und National Bank, in July. The states of Central Europe, Hungary, Czechoslovakia, Romania and Poland, all suffered heavily as outside investors called their money home.

The volume of world trade continued to fall, from 1,839 million gold dollars in December 1930 to 1,206 million dollars per month a year later.

National Government in Britain

IN JULY RAMSAY MACDONALD, Prime Minister of a Labour government, announced that major cuts would have to be made in public spending to deal with the crisis of the Depression.

MacDonald's ministers refused to support him and, in an act of desperation, MacDonald announced he was forming a new National Government, made up of the Conservative and Liberal parties, together with those members of the Labour Party who would continue to support him. Very few agreed to do so.

In October, a general election was called. The National Government swept to victory with 554 seats, of which 473 were Conservative and only 13 Labour. The main body of the Labour Party, which had refused to support MacDonald's cuts, gained only 52 seats. They never forgave MacDonald for abandoning them.

Spain becomes republic

KING ALFONSO XIII left Spain in a hurry when elections in April showed how widely unpopular the Spanish monarchy had become. From 1923 to 1930 Alfonso had supported the military dictatorship of General Primo de Rivera, but when Primo de Rivera fell from power the monarchy was doomed. A republican government took over, launched a massive school-building programme, relief programmes for the poor in the countryside and promised land reform and a reduction in the power of the Catholic Church. Many hoped that it would bring stability and justice to Spain.

Ramsay MacDonald broadcasts to the nation during the economic and political crisis of August 1931.

Cuts cause naval mutiny

IN SEPTEMBER the National Government announced that Britain would come off the gold standard, that is the value of the pound would no longer be tied to the price of gold. Instead the pound would find its own lower value, making British goods cheaper in the world's markets. Twenty-five other nations followed Britain in abandoning the gold standard.

Major cuts in public spending were also announced, amounting to a total of £70 million. The cuts were to be made in education, the armed forces and health. Unemployment benefit was to be cut by ten per cent and would not be paid after 26 weeks, except in cases of urgent need.

At Invergordon in Scotland there was a mutiny in British Navy ships when sailors heard they would have to accept cuts of 20 per cent in pay, while many senior officers would only lose 10 per cent. The mutiny spread to 12,000 sailors on 15 ships, and for two days the ships were prevented from sailing. The crisis was brought to an end when it was agreed to cut all wages equally by 10 per cent.

Dominions 'freed'

THE STATUTE OF WESTMINSTER, passed in November, allowed the British Dominions of Canada, Australia, New Zealand, Ireland and South Africa the freedom to pass their own laws without interference from the British Parliament. No law passed by the British Parliament would affect them unless they requested it. The Dominions continued to accept the British Crown as a symbol of the common links between them.

Horror movies the flavour of the year

'IT WILL CHILL YOU and fill you with fears. You'll find it creepy and cruel and crazed'. So the *New York Times* warned its readers about the film, *Dracula*, out this year. Dracula, a vampire who sucks blood from his victims, was joined in the same year by *Frankenstein*, the story of a monster created in a laboratory from human corpses. These two films started off a whole series of similar horror movies.

Meanwhile, Charlie Chaplin had another box office hit with *City Lights*, the story of a tramp who falls in love with a blind flower girl and who tries to raise money for an operation to give her back her sight. Chaplin refused to follow the fashion for talkies and provided only background music for *City Lights*.

Greyhound racing ever more popular

GREYHOUND RACING had become one of the most popular British pastimes. London alone had 17 tracks, and the estimated total attendance for 1931 was 18 million. It was estimated that a tenth of all betting was on the 'dogs'. There were 60,000 dogs registered with 30,000 owners.

Outrage at new sculpture

THE WORK OF A YORKSHIRE SCULPTOR, Henry Moore, exhibited in a one-man show at the Leicester Galleries in London, was violently criticized in the press and elsewhere. The *Morning Post* even apologized to its readers for publishing a photograph of one of the works.

Hiking boosted by youth hostels

Once I tore around the country on a motor-bike
Now I like to stretch my legs and go for a hike . . . .

A popular song of this year, 'I'm happy when I'm hiking', expressed the new enthusiasm for walking and exploring the remoter areas of Britain. The Youth Hostel Association had been founded the year before. For a yearly membership fee of 2s 6d, you could stay at a youth hostel for 6d a night if you were under eighteen and a shilling a night if you were over. The only requirement was that you had to arrive on foot or by bicycle.

Cavalcade, British stage hit of the year

Let's drink to the hope that this country of ours which we love so much will find dignity and greatness and peace again.

The final words of Noel Coward's *Cavalcade*, a scrapbook of scenes and songs of the previous 30 years, brought a tremendous ovation from the audience on the first night. At a time of gloom over the economic crisis, there was a deep longing for reassurance about the future of Britain and *Cavalcade* responded to that mood. It ran for 404 performances.

Yehudi Menuhin, the extraordinary boy violinist, was now studying and playing in Europe.

Brilliant young violinist wins top prize

A 15-YEAR-OLD VIOLINIST called Yehudi Menuhin carried off the first prize of the *Conservatoire National de France*. Born to a Jewish family in New York and spending his early years in San Francisco, Menuhin had already travelled widely and been acclaimed for his brilliant playing.

Over 35 million telephones

THE NUMBER OF TELEPHONES in the world at the beginning of 1931 was estimated to be 35,500,000. Over 21 million were in North America and over 10 million in Europe. Meanwhile, it was announced in the Soviet Union that 500,000 of the population of 150 million had access to a radio set.

Experiments in television continue

EXPERIMENTS IN TELEVISION continued on both sides of the Atlantic. In New York pictures were transmitted over three miles and it was suggested that television would be of most use to deaf people who would now be able to communicate by sign language over long distances. Meanwhile, the BBC was working with the inventor John Logie Baird and producing images made up of 30 lines to a picture. However, these were rapidly being surpassed by rival schemes such as those pioneered by Electrical and Musical Industries (EMI) which used more advanced electronic equipment and could therefore produce much clearer pictures.

Empire State Building opened

THE WORLD'S TALLEST BUILDING was opened on 1 May by President Hoover in New York. It was 380 metres high and had 102 storeys and a steel frame.

The Austin 'Seven' was first launched in 1922, but continued to be enormously popular throughout the 1930s. Bought for its value for money, reliability and the long life of its engine, by the time production ceased in 1938 over 250,000 had been built.

New speed records

A GERMAN propellor-driven Kruckenberg engine set a new record for rail speed of 143 miles per hour on 21 June, finally beating the record of 130 miles per hour set by another German train back in 1903.

On Lake Garda, in Italy, a new speedboat record of 110 miles per hour was set by Kaye Don in his boat *Miss England II*. On a later record-breaking attempt in the USA, *Miss England II* disappeared under water at high speed. Kaye Don and his co-driver were, however, saved.

The British driver Malcolm Campbell set a new land speed record of 245 miles per hour in *Blue Bird* on Daytona Beach in the USA.

George Stainforth broke the air speed record twice in 15 days in his Supermarine, powered by Rolls Royce engines. His final top speed was 408.8 miles per hour.

The new American airship, the Akron, set a record of 207 for the most passengers carried in a single airship.

A new altitude record for a manned balloon of 52,462 feet (15,990 metres) was set by two Swiss scientists, while a Dr Beebe of New York set a new deep sea diving record of 1,660 feet (506 metres).

World trade slumps

THIS WAS THE WORST YEAR of the Great Depression. As spending power dropped and most nations erected tariffs to protect their own industries against goods from overseas, world trade slumped even further. The exports of many producers of raw materials, including Chile, China, Bolivia, Cuba, Malaya, Peru and El Salvador, had fallen by over 70 per cent since 1929. Australia and New Zealand saw their exports cut by 50 per cent. The millions of unemployed suffered appallingly as governments were unable or unwilling to help them. The shock of the Depression was partic-ularly deeply felt in the USA.

Percentages of working people unemployed in 1932
Great Britain 21.9
Australia 29.0
Canada 22.0
Germany 30.1
USA 23.8
Sweden 22.8

World trade for the month of December 1932: 992 million US gold dollars, compared to 2,998 million dollars in January 1929.

'In Hoover we trusted, now we are busted'

IN THE USA feelings against President Hoover rose high among the unemployed. Hoover had no policies to deal with the Depression other than raising tariffs against foreign imports. This only made matters worse as other nations blocked the import of American goods in return.

In July Hoover ordered troops to disperse a group of unemployed ex-soldiers from the First World War who had come to Washington to ask for help. There were a hundred casualties when tanks, guns and tear-gas were used against them. Hoover's name began to be used to describe items used by the homeless poor. Hoovervilles were the shanty towns of cardboard and tin in which the homeless sheltered, Hoover bags, sacks in which belongings were carried, Hoover blankets, old newspapers to sleep in.

This 'Hoover' village was set up in the middle of New York's Central Park.

In desperation men sought any kind of work. 'Combers' would try to fish out coins which had been dropped through gratings.

rock bottom

Two million Americans on the road

AN ESTIMATED 2 MILLION Americans were reported to be on the roads looking for work in 1932. The *New York Times* reported,

Every group in society is represented in their ranks, from the college graduate to the child who has never seen the inside of a school house. Expectant mothers, sick babies, young childless couples, grimfaced middle aged dislodged from lifetime jobs – on they go, an index of insecurity in a country unused to the unexpected. We think of nomads of the desert, now we have nomads of the depression.

More Depression news from the USA

BY 1932, INVESTORS had lost 74 billion dollars on the Stock Exchange, three times the amount the USA had spent on the First World War. Five thousand banks had failed and 86,000 businesses had closed down.

The South Pacific Railway threw 683,000 passengers off its trains in 12 months for travelling without tickets.

Amtorg, the Russian trading agency in New York, was getting 350 applications a day from unemployed Americans wanting to move to Russia. One advertisement for 6,000 skilled workers got 100,000 replies.

In September, *Fortune* magazine estimated that 34 million men, women and children, 28 per cent of the population, had no income other than what they could get from begging, charity handouts and limited public welfare. This did not include America's 11 million farmers who had been devastated by drought and food prices which were so low it was often not worth moving goods to market.

In New York 20 per cent of school children were reported to be suffering from malnutrition.

The number of cars sold in the USA dropped from 4.5 million in 1929 to 1 million in 1932.

Cinema attendances were down to 60 million a week compared to 110 million in 1930.

Industry falls silent

Get there if you can and see the land you
    were once proud to own.
Though the roads have almost vanished and
    the expresses never run
Smokeless chimneys, damaged bridges,
    rotting wharves and choked canals,
Tramlines buckled, smashed trucks lying on
    their sides across the rails
Power-stations locked, deserted since they
    drew the boiler fires,
Pylons fallen or subsiding, trailing dead
    high tension wires;
Head gears gaunt on grass-grown pit-banks,
    seams abandoned years ago;
Drop a stone to listen for its splash in flooded
    dark below.
Squeeze into the works through broken
    windows or through damp-sprung doors;
See the rotted shafting, see holes gaping
    in the upper floors.

From the play, *The Dog Beneath the Skin*, by the British poet, W.H. Auden (April 1935).

Means Test bitterly resented

It is inhuman, it is horrible . . . . People who are already clinging with their teeth and fingernails to the edge of the chasm are to be formally and legally kicked into the chasm . . . .

This was British writer G.K. Chesterton's opinion of the Means Test which came fully into force in Britain in this year.

Under the cuts of 1931 unemployment benefit was only to be given for 26 weeks. After this anyone who wanted extra relief had to go through the Means Test. The household was visited and any form of income had to be declared as well as any savings. These visits with their prying questions were deeply resented by those already depressed by unemployment. Only half of those who applied were granted the maximum payment of 15s 3d a week, and within a year 180,000 had lost their benefits altogether when their 26 weeks had run out.

It is not surprising that when Prince George, the son of the King, visited the East End of London, he was greeted with shouts of 'Down with the Means Test . . . we want bread'. In other parts of Britain there were hunger marches and demonstrations which flared up into street battles in London in October. When jobs were advertised, thousands of applicants applied for just a handful of vacancies.

New US president

I pledge you, I pledge myself, to a new deal for the American people.

The verdict of the American people on Herbert Hoover was made clear when they elected Roosevelt as president in November. Roosevelt won 42 states, Hoover only six. It was one of the largest margins of victory every seen in American politics.

Despite being crippled by polio and almost unable to stand, Roosevelt's energetic campaign had taken him all over the USA. His personality and words promised action – a 'new deal' for America which would lift the country out of depression. His confidence and enthusiasm filled millions with hope.

Disarmament conference opens

AFTER MANY YEARS of planning by the League of Nations, a conference on disarmament finally opened in Geneva in February attended by 60 nations. The opening ceremony set a hopeful mood, and mass petitions for peace were presented by people who had lost loved ones in war.

However, the talks soon got bogged down. The French refused to reduce their armaments further unless Britain and the USA guaranteed to come to their aid in time of war. Both countries were unwilling to promise this. Meanwhile, Germany, its armed forces still restricted by the Treaty of Versailles forced on it after its defeat in the First World War, now demanded the same treatment as other nations. When refused, the Germans walked out of the conference, returning only in December.

Hunger marchers protest in anger against the Means Test. Hunger marches were a common form of protest in the Britain of the 1930s.

Manchukuo – a new state

IN FEBRUARY, the Japanese Government announced that Manchuria, taken over in 1931, was now an independent state and would be known as Manchukuo. In March the new head of state was installed. He was Pu-Yi, the last emperor of China, who had been forced from the Chinese throne when a small boy. The new 'state' remained controlled by Japan.

Elections in Germany

BY 1932 THERE WERE 6 MILLION unemployed in Germany and the country was becoming ungovernable. The Nazis, with their promises to revive the economy and restore the shattered greatness of Germany, appealed to almost every social class. Their brilliantly organized rallies, the magnetism of Hitler as a speaker, and the impression of strength and action that they gave convinced many that only they could solve Germany's problems.

In April Hitler challenged President Hindenburg in the presidential election and won over 13 million votes against Hindenburg's 19.5 million. In July, in the elections for the Reichstag, the Nazis became the largest party with 230 of the 608 seats and nearly 14 million of the 37 million votes cast.

However, in a new election in November, the Nazis lost 2 million votes and 34 seats. It was the Communists who gained, moving up to 100 seats. Many felt that the Nazis would now fade away. However, the new chancellor, General Schleicher, had no party and little popular support. It seemed improbable that Hitler could be kept out of power for ever.

Five Year Plan completed in four years

We are fifty to a hundred years behind the advanced countries. We must make good this lag in ten years. Either we do it or they crush us.

When Stalin spoke these words to a group of managers in February 1931 the first Five Year Plan was well under way. Now at the end of 1932 it was announced that the targets of the plan had been reached, a year ahead of schedule.

It was not true, of course, although the achievements had been remarkable. Electrical power had been trebled and coal and iron production had been doubled, but these figures were well below the targets set. Steel production was the weakest area, having risen by only a third when an increase of two and a half times had been set.

Everything else had been sacrificed to meet the targets. Workers were crammed into poorly constructed homes in the growing industrial centres. In many cases they had no industrial skills and there was widespread waste and mismanagement. Many visitors from overseas, however, believed the propaganda that a new society was being created in the Soviet Union, a striking contrast to the depressed and failed capitalist system in the west.

British Fascist Party is born

ON 1 OCTOBER Oswald Mosley, borrowing ideas and money from Benito Mussolini, the Fascist dictator of Italy, launched the British Union of Fascists.

Fascism is the greatest constructive and revolutionary creed in the world,

he proclaimed in his book *The Greater Britain*. He claimed that Britain was in decay and only a determined programme of national revival could save it.

The Fascists combined mass meetings, the first taking place in Trafalgar Square on 15 October, with parades of their marching units, the Blackshirts. The energy of the party was focused on Mosley himself who was built up as a supreme leader. Soon, however, the party was arousing distrust among those who believed its activities would inevitably lead to violence.

Fascism, British style. Oswald Mosley, leader of the British Union of Fascists, takes the salute from his followers. Mosley never attracted more than a small following.

USA tops Olympic medals table

THE OLYMPIC GAMES provided a boost for the USA in this year of depression. Held in Los Angeles, the Games were well attended, despite the vast distances many of the contestants had to travel to get there. The USA won 16 of the 29 gold medals for athletics and all 12 diving medals. The star of the Games was an 18-year-old typist from Texas, Mildred Didrikson. She won golds in the 80 metres hurdles, with a world record time, and the javelin, and was second in the high jump.

Brave – or frightening – New World?

THE MOST TALKED ABOUT BOOK of the year in Britain was *Brave New World* by Aldous Huxley. It describes a future society in which all individual freedom is crushed as human beings are graded according to their ability and conditioned to work as slaves for the state. Drugs, sex and trips to the cinema help to keep everyone happy until an outsider, a 'savage' from a reservation, visits the new society and challenges its beliefs.

Scarface – the classic gangster film

IN THE USA the early 1930s were the years of the gangsters, many of whom were making fortunes out of dealing in alcohol, forbidden under the Prohibition laws. The leading gangsters, such as Al Capone and Jack Diamond, were household names and new words such as 'racket', 'bumped off' and 'taken for a ride' came into the language.

Hollywood could not miss the opportunity. Perhaps the greatest gangster film of them all, *Scarface*, directed by Howard Hawks, appeared in 1932. Loosely based on the career of Al Capone, it tells the story of the rise and fall of a Chicago gangster called Tony Camonte.

'Hoovers' were now becoming increasingly popular in the middle-class British household, and the Hoover factory with its Art Deco style represented the latest in architectural design.

New British buildings

THE VARIETY OF STYLES in British architecture could be seen in new buildings opened in Britain this year. The BBC opened its new headquarters in Portland Place. The building cost £350,000 and was described by one writer as 'a great white ship moored in Portland Place'. Meanwhile, in Stratford, the new Shakespeare Memorial Theatre was opened on 23 April, Shakespeare's birthday. The earlier theatre had been burnt down. The new theatre was widely criticized for its dull exterior but the architect, Elizabeth Scott, said she was only concerned with providing a proper setting for plays.

Art Deco was the inspiration for the Hoover Building at Perivale in West London, while the Daily Express chose glass for its new offices in Fleet Street.

The first Royal Christmas message was broadcast by King George V to the people of the British Empire.

Empire Service launched

'DISTANT LANDS THRILL to his God Bless You' was the headline in the *New York Times* when the BBC's Empire Service went into operation in December 1932, and one of the first broadcasts was by the King, George V, who sent a Christmas message to his people across the world.

Through one of the marvels of modern science, I am enabled this Christmas Day to speak to all my people throughout the Empire . . . I speak now from my home and from my heart to you all, to men and women so cut off by the snows and deserts or the seas that only voices out of the air can reach them.

Malcolm Campbell does it again

MALCOLM CAMPBELL, who had been knighted after his record breaking run of 246 miles per hour in 1931, broke his own record again and became the first man on land to reach 250 miles per hour. The new record of 253 miles per hour was set at Daytona Beach in the USA.

World's longest single arch bridge opens

THE HARBOUR BRIDGE in Sydney, Australia, was opened this year. With a span of 1,650 feet (503 metres) it was the largest single arch bridge in the world.

Cambridge leads the world in atomic physics

UNDER THE LEADERSHIP of Ernest Rutherford, one of the great figures of modern science, the Cavendish Laboratory at Cambridge University remained the centre of developments in atomic physics, and 1932 was its greatest year. James Chadwick discovered the neutron. Neutrons, together with protons, make up the most part of every atom. Meanwhile, for the first time, two young scientists, John Cockcroft and Ernest Walton, managed to split the atom.

The science correspondent of the *Daily Herald* described a visit to the laboratory.

Rutherford led me to the high-voltage lab. It was a darkened room. Generators were humming, air pumps were throbbing. Man-made lightning crackled and flashed as the high tension spheres sparked. A tall glass pillar glowed with a luminous blue haze. Then came a clicking sound: a counter, like a mileage recorder in a motor-car, began to clock in the fragments of the splitting atoms.

The nuclear age had begun.

Woman aviators set new records

AMY JOHNSON was in the news again, flying alone from London to South Africa, setting a new record of four days and seven hours. Imperial Airways started the first regular service from London to Capetown, South Africa, in this year.

Meanwhile, an American, Amelia Earhart, who had become the first woman ever to cross the Atlantic by plane (although only as a passenger) in 1928, did it on her own in May when she set a new record for a solo crossing.

1933 Hitler comes

Hitler appointed Chancellor

ON 30 JANUARY, Adolf Hitler finally became Chancellor of Germany. The German President, the 85-year-old First World War hero, Hindenburg, had to accept Hitler and two other Nazis as ministers in a new government after the collapse of the government of General Schleicher. Hitler, however, quickly showed he intended to use his position to grab control of the state and firmly install the Nazi Party in power. By the end of 1933, Hitler was well in control.

Enabling law passed

FOLLOWING A NEW ELECTION of 5 March, in which the Nazis won 45 per cent of the votes, the new German Parliament was opened in an impressive ceremony on 21 March. It had to meet in the Kroll Opera House in Berlin following the destruction of the Reichstag building in the fire of 27 February.

Hitler knew what he wanted: a law enabling him to rule without the Reichstag. To pass such a law he needed a two-thirds majority. He achieved this by stopping the elected Communist members from sitting and by bullying the Centre party into giving him their support. Only the Social Democratic Party opposed the law but they were not strong enough to stop it being passed. From this time on, the Reichstag had no influence in German political life.

The enabling act was to last for four years and could be renewed. It marked the real beginning of the Nazi dictatorship.

On 23 June the Social Democratic Party, the largest after the Nazis, was forced to close down. In July the Nazis declared themselves the only legal party. Germany was now a one party state.

Reichstag building burns down

ON THE NIGHT OF 27 FEBRUARY the great building of the Reichstag, the German Parliament, went up in flames. Nazi leaders, who happened to be dining nearby, rushed to the scene where police held a Dutchman, Marinus van der Lubbe, who had confessed to the crime. It was claimed that Van der Lubbe had been in league with German Communists and the next day, under pressure from Hitler, President Hindenburg issued an emergency decree banning the Communist Party. In fact, 4,000 Communists had already been rounded up by dawn on the 28th.

Ever since the fire, there have been claims that the Nazis themselves were responsible for starting the fire, in order to give themselves an excuse for dealing with the Communists. It certainly came at an ideal time for them

and allowed them to deal effectively with the party which offered the most disciplined opposition to Nazism.

Van der Lubbe was later executed.

Communist banners are seized and burned by the SS.

to power

Jews fear for their lives

HITLER AND THE OTHER NAZI leaders had never hidden their obsessive contempt for the Jewish people. They were blamed for Germany's loss of the First World War, for its economic weakness and for encouraging decadent modern art.

As soon as Hitler became Chancellor there was an outburst of anti-Jewish feeling among his supporters with window smashing and public assaults and humiliations of Jews in the streets. Although these attacks were brought under control, in April the government announced a three-day boycott of Jewish businesses. On 7 April the 'Law for the Restoration of the Professional Civil Service' was passed, allowing the government to remove Jews and others who were politically unreliable from the civil service. Already thousands of Jews were being forced to consider whether they should leave their homeland and try to make new lives overseas.

Germany leaves the League

MANY WERE NOW ASKING what Germany's foreign policy would be now that Hitler was in power. Germany was still economically and militarily weak but would the new Chancellor rebuild the country's strength and launch a policy of aggression once he was strong enough to do so? This certainly seemed to be the message of his book, *Mein Kampf*, which was now becoming compulsory reading for all good Nazis.

In a speech of 17 May Hitler claimed that he only wanted peace. He said he was prepared to renounce offensive weapons and to allow inspection of military operations in Germany. However, in October he announced that Germany was walking out of the disarmament conference and leaving the League of Nations. The disarmament conference was not prepared to allow Germany the freedom to build up its armies to the size of other nations while the League, Hitler claimed, really only represented the victors of the First World War and gave Germany a second-class status he was not prepared to accept. He got overwhelming support in Germany for his moves. The disarmament conference broke up soon afterwards and never met again.

A boycott of Jewish shops in Germany gave the first ominous sign of where Nazism would lead.

World News

President Roosevelt gets to work

This is pre-eminently the time to speak the truth, the whole truth, frankly and boldly. Nor need we shrink from honestly facing conditions in our country today. This great nation will endure as it has endured, will revive and will prosper.

So first of all let me assert my firm belief that the only thing we have to fear is fear itself – nameless, unreasoning, unjustified terror which paralyses needed effort to convert retreat into advance.

Our greatest primary task is to get people to work. This is no unsolvable problem if we face it wisely and courageously.

Franklin Roosevelt's speech, delivered at his inauguration as President on 4 March, raised the hopes of America. Within 100 days a mass of laws had been passed by Congress to help get the nation moving again. A banking act closed down the weaker banks restoring confidence in the rest and encouraging investors to bring their money back. The Civilian Conservation Corps found work for 250,000 of the young unemployed, building dams and draining marshes. Farmers were helped to pay off their debts and the Federal Emergency Relief Act gave out $500 million for the relief of the poor. All kinds of public works projects were funded in order to provide employment and to improve the nation's schools, roads and hospitals. The Tennessee Valley Authority was set up in one of the most poverty-stricken states, using the Tennessee River to generate cheap electricity. Thousands of jobs were created as dams were built and power lines extended through the valley.

Despite all the enthusiasm and hope, unemployment remained high. The country still waited to see whether the 'new deal' would really bring back prosperity.

'Nothing to fear but fear itself': the newly elected American President, Franklin Roosevelt, brought a new spirit to the fight to overcome the Depression.

Famine in Russia

BY 1933 STORIES were reaching the West that a dreadful famine had struck Central European Russia with estimates of up to 6 million deaths.

In 1932 Stalin had ordered a further move towards collective farms, although this time peasants were to be allowed to have small plots of their own land, keep poultry and some of their own farming tools. Some 50 per cent of the rural population were in farms by the end of the year. However, the harvest of 1932 had been a disaster and the result was starvation. The state did little to help.

All had travelled in the flat country and beyond Odessa and they reported that the further they went the greater was the misery. They spoke of starved children with swollen abdomens who were seen along the railway tracks, not occasionally but as a common spectacle, of fieldmice being in demand for food and of thousands unable to work from undernourishment and being therefore deprived of rations on the grounds of laziness.
(Reports of interviews with travellers to more remote parts of Russia in the *New York Times*)

Meanwhile a second Five Year Plan had begun. Once again it was to concentrate on heavy industry with high targets set for coal, iron, steel and electrical power.

Spanish Republic runs into trouble

THE SPANISH REPUBLIC, founded with high hopes in 1931, was in trouble by 1933. The Catholic Church was infuriated by laws which reduced its influence and allowed divorce. The army was resentful of new laws which allowed the army to be attacked in the press and the government's policy of land reform only aroused widespread unrest in the countryside. In November elections brought success for right-wing parties which backed the Church and the army. Their success was met by a Communist uprising a month later which, however, failed. Increasingly, Spain was becoming split into rival and bitterly opposed groups.

Gandhi continues to infuriate the British

THE BRITISH GOVERNMENT in India was still at a loss as to how to handle the Indian nationalist leader Gandhi. He was imprisoned for much of 1932 and then again in 1933. On both these occasions he launched hunger strikes to further his campaign for equal treatment for the Untouchables, the lowest caste of Hindus who were shunned by the higher castes. In August 1933 he had to be released after he came near to death. The British simply could not afford to have him die while in one of their prisons and they knew he had the will to fast to death. In November, free again, Gandhi started a tour of every province in India to learn more about the conditions of the Untouchables.

Japan leaves the League

LORD LYTTON'S COMMISSION reached Japan in March 1932, four and a half months after the invasion of Manchuria. The commission went on to spend six weeks in Manchuria before publishing a 400 page report in October. While accepting that the Chinese had been provocative towards Japan, the report blamed the Japanese for their aggression and takeover of Manchuria.

The report was debated by a special assembly of the League in February 1933 and Japan was the only one of the 42 nations present to vote against a motion condemning the takeover. The Japanese left the League in disgust and nothing was ever done to punish them for their aggression.

Three million unemployed

IN JANUARY 1933, unemployment in Britain reached its highest recorded figure, 2,979,000. In *Love on the Dole*, published this year, Walter Greenwood, a working man himself, described the effects of long-term unemployment, calling it a 'malignant disease'.

Arts fall under Nazi control

THE WORLD-FAMOUS Bauhaus School of Design was one of the many institutions to fall victim to the Nazis in 1933. A centre of training and experiment in new ideas in art, it was forced to close as the Nazis launched a campaign against modern art. Many of its teachers fled abroad.

The Nazi regime rooted out Jewish artists and writers and directed that all art should be guided by 'German traditions'. In May enormous bonfires of 'un-German' books were burned in Berlin and Munich. The literature section of the famous Prussian Academy of Arts saw half its members expelled by the end of 1933. The foremost German novelist, Thomas Mann, refused to return home to Germany in protest. The communist writer, Bertolt Brecht, also went into exile.

The Nazi Propaganda Minister Josef Goebbels was fully aware of the importance of using the cinema, and the regime was soon engaged in propaganda films, such as those of Leni Riefenstahl.

The Australian batsman, Fingleton, ducks as he faces a ball from Harry Larwood, the English fast bowler.

Bodyline controversy rocks world cricket

TELEGRAM FROM THE AUSTRALIAN Board of Control for Cricket to the MCC, 17 January, 1933.

Body-line bowling has assumed such proportions as to menace the best interests of the game, making protection of the body by the batsmen the main consideration . . . . This is causing intensely bitter feeling between the players as well as injury. In our opinion it is unsportsmanlike.

Telegram from the MCC to the Australian Board of Control, 24 January, 1933.

We, the Marylebone Cricket Club, deplore your cable. We deprecate your opinion that there has been unsportsmanlike play. We have the fullest confidence in captain, team and managers and are convinced that they would do nothing to infringe either the laws of cricket or the spirit of the game!

The great bodyline controversy broke out at the Third Test between England and Australia in Adelaide. So far the series had gone well, each team winning a match. However, on the third day of the match, when Australia were batting, the English fast bowler, Larwood, appeared to start bowling straight at the batsman. Two Australian batsmen, Woodfull and Oldfield, were forced to leave the field after being hit and it was later found that Oldfield had suffered a cracked skull. By the end of the day the Australian crowd was outraged and the next day the Australian Board of Control sent a protest to the MCC.

The story spread to every cricketing part of the British Empire and there was an intense debate as to whether bodyline bowling was justified. The English team moved round Australia under a cloud of suspicion and many believed the series should end and the team return home. However, the Fourth Test did get under way. Larwood continued his bodyline bowling, but this time the Australian batsmen had learned how to cope with it. The bodyline controversy died down almost as quickly as it had begun.

New super-cinema

A BIRMINGHAM scrap-metal merchant, Oscar Deutsch, founded a new chain of cinemas in 1933. They were all called the Odeon and represented the latest in modern taste and luxury. The Odeon chain rivalled the two other cinema chains in Britain, Gaumont British and Associated British Cinemas (ABC).

Hollywood cheers up the world

BY 1933 THE GREAT STUDIOS of Hollywood were churning out spectacular musicals to which the poor flocked for a glimpse of another world. At Warner Brothers Busby Berkeley used extravagant costumes, aerial photography and sophisticated editing for his backstage romances such as *42nd Street, Gold Diggers of 1933* and *Footlight Parade*.

The film *Flying Down to Rio* was a major success for its dancing co-stars, Ginger Rogers and Fred Astaire, and set them off on one of the most successful dancing partnerships of all time. Another big success of 1933 was *King Kong* from the RKO Studio, a brilliantly constructed film in which a city is terrorized by a monster ape.

The first British film to break into the American market was Alexander Korda's *The Private Life of Henry VIII*, starring Charles Laughton. It started off a whole series of historical biographies.

Science books popular

BOOKS EXPLAINING the developments in modern science were becoming increasingly popular with the British public. H.G. Wells, the novelist, took on a new role as the educator of the public in science, with books such as *The Science of Life* (1931) and, in 1933, *The Shape of Things to Come*. *The Shape of Things to Come* gave a gloomy picture of the impact of science on modern civilization predicting, among other things, mass destruction caused by aerial bombing. Another educational book of 1933 was Sir Arthur Eddington's *The Expanding Universe* which explained developments in astronomy.

Albert Einstein, the world famous nuclear physicist, left Germany in 1933 to go to the USA. He was a bitter opponent of Nazism and gave much help to other refugees from Nazi persecution.

Einstein warns of coming war

SCIENTISTS INCREASINGLY FELT they had a duty to warn the public of dangers to come. Albert Einstein, one of the most brilliant scientists of all time, whose books were being burnt in Germany and who had renounced his German citizenship in 1933, issued a warning at a mass meeting at the Albert Hall in London:

How can we save mankind and its spiritual acquisitions of which we are the heirs? The Great War and the privations of the people resulting from it are in some measure responsible for the present dangerous upheavals. Discontent breeds hatred, and hatred leads to acts of violence and revolution, and often war.

Already he was convinced that Hitler was preparing for war.

It's Sir Malcolm again

SIR MALCOLM CAMPBELL was back at Daytona Beach with *Blue Bird* to carry on with his obsession to set yet another world landspeed record. Once again he succeeded and pushed the record to over 270 miles per hour.

Not up but over Mount Everest

THERE HAD BEEN SEVERAL attempts to climb Mount Everest, the world's highest mountain, in these years but all had been unsuccessful. In April, however, two British planes managed to fly over the mountain for the first time.

1934

Dictators

The Night of the Long Knives

ON 30 JUNE HITLER moved against the leaders of the Stormtroopers (the SA), the organization of 2 million men which provided the massed ranks at so many Nazi ceremonies. Their leader Rohm was hauled out of bed in a hotel near Munich by Hitler himself and sent off to be shot. Dozens of other SA leaders followed him and the opportunity was also taken to get rid of other old rivals, including the Chancellor Hitler had replaced in January 1933, General von Schleicher. Perhaps 150 to 200 people died.

Hitler claimed that there had been a plot against him and that he had been forced to take the law into his own hands in order to defend the state against attack. It marked a sinister moment, the moment that Hitler showed he lacked any interest in law or humanity.

Meanwhile, in the Soviet Union, after the mysterious murder of Sergei Kirov, the Communist Party leader in Leningrad, Stalin also launched a campaign of terror against his opponents. Dictatorship was developing in new and nasty ways.

SS gets more power

THE BRUTAL KILLINGS of 30 June had been carried out by the SS. The SS had originally been formed as Hitler's bodyguard but under its leader Heinrich Himmler, it soon developed into something very different. Himmler saw the SS as an elite group, perfectly disciplined, made up of only the most loyal Nazis. He developed it so successfully that Hitler gave the SS greater and greater power. It became increasingly concerned with maintaining Nazi racial policies, dealing with enemies of the state and, most sinisterly of all, with running the concentration camps. By 1934 the SS was subject to few rules, except those of its own making.

The army supports Hitler as he becomes the Führer

MANY SENIOR OFFICERS in the German army had been suspicious of Hitler. After all he had been a mere corporal in the First World War. They feared that he might allow the SA to develop into an undisciplined armed force which would rival their power. The army was thus delighted when Hitler decided to crush the SA and they even provided the transport which the SS executioners used for their brutal job. Afterwards many leading generals came forward to congratulate Hitler for saving the state.

On 2 August, the old President Hindenburg died. Hitler announced that he was joining Hindenburg's powers with his own and would now have the title Führer or Leader. The army accepted him as their Commander-in-Chief and every soldier had to swear an oath of personal loyalty to him.

I swear by God this sacred oath, that I will yield unconditional obedience to the Führer of the German Reich and Volk, Adolf Hitler . . . and, as a brave soldier, will be ready at any time to lay down my life for this oath.

Stormtroopers looking for power?

THE STORMTROOPERS (*Sturmabteilung* or *SA* in German) were well known to the cinema audiences of Europe who had seen them in the newsreels, marching and parading at Nazi ceremonies. There were some 2 million of them by 1934 but many were frustrated. When the Nazis came to power they had hoped for jobs and power in the new government. Their leader Ernst Rohm talked of their becoming a new mass army. Other Nazi leaders and army generals fearful of the chaos that would follow if the SA was given power fed Hitler stories of plots against him. Finally, Hitler decided to act and crush the SA as a dangerous force once and for all. This is what happened on the night of 30 June.

crush rivals

Adolf Hitler, now the Führer, was in firm control of Germany by 1934.

Hitler addresses the faithful. The individual is lost in the mass.

Kirov slain

The first assassination of an important political figure in the Soviet Union since 1918 occurred at 4.30pm today. The victim was Sergei Kirov, a member of the Politburo of the Communist Party, the group of ten which is the real ruling power of the Soviet Union.

Mr. Kirov was shot and killed in the quarters of the Leningrad Committee of the Communist Party . . . few details have been given out. It was merely said that the assassination had been 'instigated by enemies of the working class'. The murderer has been arrested and his identity is being sought.
(The *New York Times* reporting from Moscow, 1 December)

The murder of Sergei Kirov has remained surrounded by mystery. Kirov was a popular leader, good-looking, a powerful speaker and, unlike Stalin who came from the southern state of Georgia, a Russian. It was rumoured that at the Party Conference of 1934 there had been an attempt to elect Kirov to the top post of General Secretary in place of Stalin.

Suspicious circumstances surrounded the killing. Kirov's assassin, Nikolaev, had been arrested in the Party head-quarters twice before with a revolver but the police had released him. On the day of the assassination, Kirov's body-guards had been told he did not need them and the head of the guards was killed in a suspicious car accident the very next day. Stalin himself seemed ready for something and had covered the 600 kilometre journey to Leningrad by special train within a few hours of the news.

Stalin immediately issued a decree allowing him to deal with enemies of the state or 'terrorists' as they were described. Such 'terrorists' were to be arrested and dealt with swiftly with no rights of appeal. Among those arrested were two former senior leaders of the Communist Party, Zinoviev and Kamenev, who had been rivals to Stalin in the 1920s.

Terror in USSR

1934 SAW THE BEGINNING of a period of terror in the Soviet Union. The secret police force, the OGPU (hated and feared during the collectivization programme when it was responsible for the arrests of thousands of kulaks), merged with the People's Commissariat for Internal Affairs (known by the initials of its Russian name, NKVD).

Stalin was becoming obsessed by the fear of opposition and used this political police organization to arrest and imprison suspected opponents of his industrial and agricultural policies. During 1934 the number of Russian Communist Party members fell from 3.5 million to 2.7 million.

Nazis sign pact with Poland

IN JANUARY the diplomatic world was amazed to hear that Hitler had signed a ten-year non-aggression pact with Poland. The Germans had long complained that the Polish border had been unfairly drawn up at the end of the First World War with parts of the old Germany included in Poland. Many had assumed that one of Hitler's first aims would be to try to redraw the border in Germany's favour, not sign a treaty of friendship.

The move left many believing that perhaps Hitler wanted peace after all. Others noticed, however, that by drawing closer to Germany, Poland was drawing away from its ally, France. If Hitler did turn against her in the future, Poland might find itself isolated.

Spain drifts to anarchy

CONDITIONS WORSENED IN SPAIN this year as a succession of weak governments tried to keep order. There was increasing unrest, strike activity and violence both in the cities and among workers in the countryside.

In Catalonia, in northern Spain, an independent Catalan state was proclaimed in October. It was suppressed by the government and its leaders later received 30-year prison sentences.

More seriously, in the northern mining province of Asturia there was a major rebellion of miners, also in October. North African troops were called in to crush it (it was feared that Spanish troops might not fire on their own people). At least 1300 were killed and 3000 wounded in the suppression of the revolt. By the end of 1934 Spain appeared to be becoming ungovernable.

Olympia meeting dishonours British Fascism

OSWALD MOSLEY'S British Union of Fascists was severely discredited after widespread violence at a meeting held in the great hall at Olympia on 7 June. Anyone who heckled the speakers was set upon by Blackshirt stewards, beaten up and thrown out of the hall. There was a great deal of publicity following this violence, and the movement lost much of what little support it had won.

USSR joins League of Nations

THE SOVIET LEADER STALIN had never shown much respect for the League of Nations, on one occasion calling it 'a rotting corpse'. However, by 1934 Stalin was becoming seriously concerned about the rising power of Germany. He remembered only too well the successful and humiliating German invasion of Russia in the First World War and feared it could happen again.

Stalin realized he could not risk being isolated in the event of a German attack and needed to build better relations with anti-Hitler nations. As a first step the Soviet Union applied for membership of the League of Nations. In September, the Council of the League voted unanimously to admit it.

Stavisky scandal

FRANCE SAW A MARKED decline in its strength in the early 1930s. The Depression came later there than it did in other nations – the worst year was 1934 when other countries were already starting to recover. Vulnerable to a strong Germany, France had most to lose from the rise of Hitler and the failure of the League of Nations. Worse still it could not find a stable government. There were four cabinets in just 15 months between December 1932 and February 1934, and the politicians in the Chambers, where the power really lay, seemed unable to consider either reform or a strong foreign policy.

The reported suicide of a crooked financier, Stavisky, in October 1933 aroused a mass of discontent. Many believed that Stavisky had been killed simply to stop him revealing scandalous details of the corruption of leading politicians. There were massive demon-strations in Paris and at one of these, on 6 February, 14 people were killed and over 600 wounded as demonstrators tried to break through to the Chamber of Deputies.

A Government of National Union was eventually set up and the unrest died down but no government in France in the 1930s was to find the political and economic strength to face the rising power of Germany.

Long March begins

ONE OF THE MOST EPIC journeys in history began in China in October. Chinese Communist guerillas had found that their base in the south-east province of Kiangsi was being gradually surrounded by the troops of the nationalist government under Chiang Kaishek. The Communists decided to break out and take their forces westwards and then north to a more remote area of China where they could be safe.

Mao Zedong emerged as leader of the Chinese Communists during the extraordinary Long March of 1934 to 1935.

Nazis attempt coup in Austria

THE AUSTRIAN GOVERNMENT came close to being overthrown at the hands of Nazis in July. The Chancellor, Dollfuss, who had come to power as a dictator only three months before, was killed in the uprising.

The Austrian Nazis were believed to have had the backing of Hitler in this attempt. However, when the coup failed Hitler pretended he had known nothing about it.

One aim of the Austrian Nazis was to unite Austria with Germany to form a larger German state. This would be a direct threat to Italy, and Mussolini sent Italian troops up to the Austrian border as a direct warning against such union (which had been forbidden anyway by the Treaty of Versailles).

Hollywood's Code of Decency

FOLLOWING INCREASED PROTEST about growing violence in American films, particularly those of gangster life, the Catholic Church and the so-called League of Decency drew up a code which all American films were supposed to follow.

No illegal weapons, such as machine guns, could be shown in a film, and criminals had to be shown to be punished. No policeman was to be shown getting killed.

Marriage was to be upheld as the only relationship in which sex was allowed, but even married couples had to be shown to have separate beds. Adultery could only be mentioned if it were vital to the plot, and only then if the adulterer was seen to suffer for his or her behaviour. There was to be no nudity. The code also forbade scenes of excessive drinking or of cruelty to animals or children.

The power of the League of Decency was such that Hollywood fell into line, and these rules lasted throughout the 1930s.

Which is the real England?

IN HIS NEW BOOK, *English Journey*, the Yorkshire author, J.B. Priestley, described four different Englands he had found as he travelled round the country. The first was the old England of sleepy villages and thatched cottages. The second was the industrial England of the north, formed in the nineteenth century and dominated by its factories and coal mines. Then there was the England of the dole and the Means Test, poor and unemployed. However, there was also a new England emerging. Priestley described it as an England of

filling stations and factories that look like exhibition buildings, of giant cinemas and dance-halls and cafes, bungalows with tiny garages, cocktail bars, Woolworths, motor-coaches, wireless, hiking, factory girls looking like actresses, greyhound racing and dirt tracks, swimming pools and everything given away for cigarette coupons.

Italy wins World Cup

BENITO MUSSOLINI, the leader of Fascist Italy, had long claimed that Fascism was building a new kind of man in Italy. The Fascists claimed that evidence was provided for this in June when Italy won the World Cup in football beating Czechoslovakia in the final 2-1. Britain was still in dispute with FIFA, which organized the Cup, and did not participate.

English triumph at Wimbledon

FOR THE FIRST TIME since 1909, English players won both the men's and women's singles titles at Wimbledon this year. Fred Perry won the men's title while Dorothy Round captured the women's title before going on to win the mixed doubles. Women were allowed to wear shorts for the first time this year.

Elgar dies

THE GREAT ENGLISH COMPOSER, Edward Elgar, died in February. Although he had composed little since 1920, his *Enigma Variations* and violin and cello concertos had become a much loved part of English music. 'Land of Hope and Glory' from the *Pomp and Circumstance Marches* was a popular event at the last night of the Proms. In 1933, in one of his last appearances, Elgar had conducted the young Yehudi Menuhin in a recorded version of his Violin Concerto.

Sir Edward Elgar, the English composer, died this year.

Queen Mary finally launched

THE LUXURY TRANSATLANTIC liner the *Queen Mary* was launched by the Queen it was named after (Queen Mary, the wife of King George V) on 26 September. It was the first ship over 75,000 tons (76,240 tonnes).

The *Queen Mary* had started life on the River Clyde on the west coast of Scotland called simply Number 534. Building work on the ship had stopped as a result of the Depression, and the hull had started to rot. Luckily, the government came to the rescue with a grant, and the liner was triumphantly finished.

Neutrons get to work

THE NEUTRON had been discovered by Chadwick in Cambridge in 1932. Now the Italian physicist Enrico Fermi experimented with neutrons, passing them through other elements in order to produce radioactive particles. He tried a number of different elements but when he came to uranium he found that new radioactive substances were being produced which he could not identify. Little did he know then that the uranium was being broken up and some of its mass being converted into a stupendous new form of energy – atomic energy.

'Loch Ness Monster filmed'

SO CLAIMED one newspaper which also said it had 'twelve humps and a mane like a horse'.

The combined talents of British scientists were called upon in 1933 and 1934 to explain sightings of a 'monster' in the Scottish Loch Ness. Most sightings were of disturbances in the water. While the popular press reported stories of people being carried off across the moors by a monster and of dead sheep found with large teeth marks, scientists suggested it was either an illusion or perhaps a whale or shark which had come into the Loch while small and been trapped when it was bigger. Meanwhile, thousands flocked to the shore of the Loch in the hope of seeing the monster, bringing major traffic jams to remote Highland roads.

Fridges big and small

FRIDGES WERE coming into common use in homes for the first time. There were still problems with freezing large quantities of food, however: deep-frozen foods deteriorated very quickly when defrosted. In 1934 a major improvement in keeping food took place when it was discovered that, by adding carbon dioxide to the air in which food was chilled rather than frozen, the food could be kept fresh for long periods and it also had a better flavour. Oxygen was added to the mixture to stop the food losing its colour when it was thawed.

Mersey Tunnel opened

THE WORLD'S LONGEST underwater tunnel, the Mersey Tunnel, was opened by King George V on 18 July. Meanwhile, a new London landmark came into being with the opening of the dominating Battersea Power Station on the south bank of the Thames.

Cookers and fridges were now becoming a standard part of the middle-class British home.

Mussolini plans attack

THE KINGDOM OF ABYSSINIA, mountainous and poor, was sandwiched between two Italian colonies, Italian Somaliland and Eritrea. Mussolini, the Fascist leader of Italy, was determined to force the country into his empire. Plans for invasion had been drawn up as early as 1933.

The world had certainly been warned. For ten months there had been border disputes between the Italians and the Abyssinians; Haile Selassie, the Emperor of Abyssinia, had appealed to the League of Nations for help against the threatening behaviour of the Italian government.

However, Mussolini was not to be put off. His regime, now in power for 13 years, was running out of steam. The Italian people had not been transformed into the united and strong community that Mussolini had promised, and their enthusiasm for his rule was beginning to fade. He desperately needed a successful foreign policy to revive the fortunes of Italy. Abyssinia, a country which had humiliated Italy by defeating its troops at the battle of Adowa in 1896, seemed an easy target, and its conquest would allow Mussolini to proclaim a new Roman Empire.

The Italians move in

ON 3 OCTOBER, the invasion began. Italian armies moved northwards from Italian Somaliland and south from the colony of Eritrea. Among the towns first attacked was that of Adowa, in revenge for the defeat of 1896. As the Italian troops encountered resistance, stories of their barbarity were soon coming out of Abyssinia; civilians were being bombed and poison gas was being used widely.

The Abyssinian army was poorly equipped and the air force had only 12 planes. Abyssinia's greatest weapon was the mountainous and remote nature of the country itself and in the south, the Italian armies were soon held up by waterlogged roads. Mussolini simply ordered a more effective use of gas and terror, successfully concealing his difficulties from the outside world.

Benito Mussolini, the Fascist dictator of Italy, saw Abyssinia as a weak country he could easily crush in his search for a new Roman Empire.

British public against aggression

IN THE SUMMER OF 1935 a peace ballot had been organized in Britain. In house-to-house visits, nearly 11 million people had been asked their views on action against aggression. The support for the League of Nations was overwhelming. Of those questioned 97 per cent said that they wished Britain to remain a member, while 87 per cent supported the use of economic sanctions by the League against any aggressor and 59 per cent were in favour of military sanctions.

The British government appeared to accept such views. In September, the Foreign Secretary, Sir Samuel Hoare, in a rousing speech to the League, said that Britain would support firm action against any aggressor.

The League condemns invasion

THE LEAGUE OF NATIONS had been discussing the disputes between Italy and Abyssinia for ten months but nothing effective had been done to stop the invasion.

In October, in a sudden burst of action, the League condemned the invasion and decided to introduce numerous economic sanctions against Italy. These included the stopping of all loans, a ban on importing goods from Italy and restrictions on some exports. However, these sanctions did not include oil, coal or steel, and there was no agreement to close the Suez Canal to Italian shipping, even though the Canal was her main supply route.

Abyssinia

Haile Selassie, here seen at his coronation as Emperor of Abyssinia in 1930, was a Christian ruler who tried to use his authority to modernize his country.

It was soon clear that without more forceful leadership from Britain and France, the League would not be able to stop Mussolini. This was a leadership which Britain and France were not willing or able to provide.

Hoare-Laval pact discredits Britain and France

WHEN THE MOMENT for action came the British government began to waver. After all, could they afford to have Italy as an enemy, just at a time when Germany and, further afield, Japan, were rearming? Strong action against Italy might just drive her into the arms of Germany and make Britain's position all the weaker.

The French saw things in the same way. Facing a rearmed Germany to the north was bad enough. Could they survive if they also had to face a hostile country, such as Italy, to their south?

In December, the two governments were ready to make a deal. Samuel Hoare, the British Foreign Secretary, on a visit to Paris, signed a secret agreement with the French Prime Minister, Pierre Laval (who also held the office of Foreign Minister), under which they would settle the Abyssinian crisis by allowing Mussolini to keep the richer parts of Abyssinia if he handed back the remainder to Emperor Haile Selassie. It was a sell-out.

However, the details were leaked in Paris. When the news of the sell-out reached Britain there was outrage among the public. This feeling was echoed in the Conservative Party, just after a general election in which the National government had campaigned on a policy of support for the League of Nations against aggression! The government had to back down and Hoare was forced to resign as Foreign Secretary. It was not a happy or honourable moment for British politics.

Worse was to come. When the French heard that the British government was backing out of the deal, all their worst fears about the untrustworthiness of the British seemed to be coming true. They had already felt betrayed by an Anglo-German Naval Agreement in June. Once again the British had let them down. Could they be trusted if there was trouble in the future?

Breach of Treaty of Versailles

ON 8 MARCH HITLER announced that the Germans already had an air force, the *Luftwaffe*, although this had been forbidden by the Treaty of Versailles. A week later he announced that he was building an army of 500,000 men, although the treaty only allowed Germany 100,000.

Britain, France and Italy met at Stresa in northern Italy to condemn the announcement, stressing that they would act together to stop any further breaches of the treaty. The following month, to the fury of Hitler, the Council of the League of Nations also condemned his moves.

Russia comes in out of the cold

STALIN, INCREASINGLY AFRAID of the rising power of Germany, strengthened the position of Russia this year by making a defence agreement with France. Czechoslovakia was also offered protection. If it were attacked, Russia would come to its help, but only if the French did so as well.

In the USA, however, things were going in the opposite direction. A series of neutrality acts, the first of which was passed this year, were designed to keep the USA out of trouble. No arms could be sold to either side in any conflict. In effect, the USA was isolating itself from world affairs.

Stresa Front breaks up

Pierre Laval, the French Prime Minister, was determined to remain friendly with Italy, even if it meant accepting Mussolini's aggression in Abyssinia. He felt bitterly betrayed by Britain after the collapse of the Hoare-Laval pact.

THE UNITY OF THE STRESA FRONT did not last long. Italy was preoccupied with the invasion of Abyssinia. In Britain there was a strong feeling that peace should be kept at any price. When Hitler cleverly suggested to the British government that Germany and Britain make a naval agreement, the British accepted, agreeing that the Germans could build a fleet up to 35 per cent of the size of the British one. In effect, Hitler had been allowed to escape from the limits of the Treaty of Versailles.

The French were furious with the British. They stood to lose more from a stronger Germany, and the British had conducted the naval agreement without any consultation with them at all. They were made even more angry later in the year by the failure of the Hoare-Laval pact.

Hitler was beginning to realize that there would be little effective opposition if he chose to expand further.

Long March ends

ONE OF THE MOST EXTRAORDINARY feats of human endurance in history ended in October this year, when 8000 Communists, all that were left of some 100,000 who had set out a year before, reached the northern Chinese province of Shensi. They had come 6000 miles, across 18 mountain ranges and 24 rivers, in search of a safe home away from the attacks of the Nationalist government of China. Disease, starva-tion and air and ground attacks by the Nationalists had worn down their numbers.

During the march a new Communist leader had emerged, Mao Zedong. Mao himself had lost his brother and two of his children on the march, but now had beaten other rivals for leader-ship and would prove unchallengeable as Communist leader from now on.

Baldwin new Prime Minister in Jubilee Year

BRITAIN SAW A NEW PRIME MINISTER take office in June. Stanley Baldwin, who had already been Prime Minister between 1924 and 1929, succeeded Ramsay MacDonald who had founded the National Government four years before. Baldwin, leader of the Conservative Party, was a calm and reassuring politician who promised continued and steady recovery from the Depression.

For the British public, however, the year had been dominated by the Silver Jubilee celebrations. King George V, now an old man, was overwhelmed by the affection his 25 years on the throne produced throughout the land. Even in the poorest areas his visits were greeted with loyal enthusiasm, including banners inscribed, 'Lousy (i.e. suffering from lice) but Loyal'.

Government of India Act

THE LONGEST, and one of the most complicated, acts in the history of the British Parliament was finally passed this year. The Government of India Act marked the first step to full independence for India, perhaps, it was believed, to be achieved by 1955.

Forty million Indians were now entitled to vote in the country's 11 provinces. This offered the chance to the Congress Party, the main force for independence, to take power at local level and achieve a position of strength from which the British would not be able to dislodge it. The princes, who still held their own states, would be able to participate in the national government of India if they chose to do so.

The act would have been passed two years earlier if it had not been for the determined opposition of a group of Conservative 'die-hards', led by Winston Churchill. 'The British lion', said Churchill scornfully, 'can now be chased by rabbits from the fields and forests of his former glory . . . we are the victims of a nervous collapse.' Despite the brilliance of many of Churchill's speeches against the act, most Conservatives felt he had become out of touch with the modern world.

Stanley Baldwin was a calm and reassuring figure as British Prime Minister, but he failed to face up to the threats posed by the military power of the dictators.

Sport and the Arts

Hitler's views on art

I am convinced that art, since it forms the most uncorrupted, the most immediate reflection of the people's soul, exercises unconsciously by far the greatest influence upon the masses of the people.
(Adolf Hitler, 1935)

One way in which the Nazi regime was reaching a wider audience was through films. Leni Riefenstahl produced *The Triumph of the Will*, a dramatic study of the 1934 Nazi Party Congress at Nuremberg, in which Hitler is portrayed as a messiah descending in his aeroplane from the clouds to meet the massed ranks of his party. The film was such an effective glorification of dictatorship that it was banned in Britain, Canada and the USA.

The Informer, top film of the year

THE MOST ACCLAIMED FILM of the year was *The Informer*, directed by John Ford, from a story by the Irish writer, Liam O'Flaherty. It tells the story of an IRA man who has betrayed a fellow member of the IRA to the British for money. He is haunted by his action and finally the IRA catch up with and kill him.

The public's attention was also caught by a new child star – Shirley Temple, aged seven in 1935. She made a fortune for her studio, Twentieth Century Fox, starring in four films in 1935 alone. An older actress, Greta Garbo, one of the few who had successfully made the transition from silent to talking films, continued her career as one of the all time cinema 'greats' with the film *Anna Karenina*.

Meanwhile, the dancing partnership of Ginger Rogers and Fred Astaire continued to draw in the crowds. After *The Gay Divorcee* in 1934 came *Top Hat* in 1935 with a big hit for the song 'Cheek to Cheek'.

Stalin to transform Moscow

THE SOVIET leader Josef Stalin finalized plans for the transformation of Moscow in 1935. The Cathedral of Christ the Saviour was to be demolished to make way for a new Palace of Soviets which was to be the largest building in the world. It was to hold 21,000 people and to carry a 6600 tonne statue of Lenin on the top. The new Moscow Metro was opened and a ten-year plan to transform the rest of the city was launched. The Palace of Soviets was never built but much of the rest of the plan was carried out.

The Birth of Swing

A NEW FASHION IN MUSIC, Swing, swept the world in 1935. Swing was born in Los Angeles one night in August 1935, when a 25-year-old band leader, Benny Goodman, experimented with a new, faster dance rythym using saxophones and drums. It caught on at once.

Fred Perry, winner of this year's Wimbledon men's singles, is seen here on the opening day of the championships.

Penguins launched

THE BRITISH PUBLISHER Allen Lane launched a daring new venture in 1935: the world's first paperback books. Known as Penguins, they sold for six pence each. Title number one was *Ariel*, a life of the poet Shelley by André Maurois, and among the first ten were *A Farewell to Arms* by Ernest Hemingway and thrillers by Dorothy Sayers and Agatha Christie. Woolworths sent in a big order and the series was soon a major success.

Sporting news

IN 1935 the horse of the year was Bahram, owned by the Aga Khan, which won the three major flat races of the racing year, the 2000 Guineas, the Derby and the St Leger.

In tennis Fred Perry won the men's singles title at Wimbledon again. The FA Cup, held as usual at Wembley Stadium, was won by Sheffield Wednesday.

Sportsmen were making their final preparations for the 1936 Olympic Games. The greatest interest was in a 21-year-old American athlete, Jesse Owens, who had smashed no less than five world records in one afternoon in May.

Radar sees in the dark

A MAJOR NEW INVENTION was demonstrated by British scientists in 1935. Robert Watson-Watt, head of the Radio Department of the National Physical Laboratory, developed a machine which could detect planes before they could be seen or heard in any other way.

He tested it out for the Air Ministry, who arranged for a bomber to be flown towards Watson-Watt and his machine, which was set up in a van. As Watson-Watt recalled:

We sat inside the van and eagerly watched the cathode-ray tube on which we should see a wiggly line if my calculations were correct. During the next few moments no one said a word. Then came a dramatic, an historic moment. The line wiggled vigorously – at that moment the aircraft was eight miles away.

The experiment had worked.

By the end of 1935 Watson-Watt, now installed at a testing station at Orfordness in Suffolk, was picking up planes 70 miles away and was able to calculate their height and direction.

Television nearly ready to go public

EXPERIMENTS IN TELEVISION continued in several countries, including the USA, Britain and Germany. However, it looked as if the BBC would be the first to get a public service going. It was clear that the electronic system pioneered by EMI and Marconi, under the leadership of Isaac Schoenberg, was now superior to the one developed by John Logie Baird. Schoenberg, a Russian physicist who had come to Britain in 1914, led the EMI-Marconi team but its most brilliant member was Alan Blumlein.

Hurricane flies for the first time

A MODEL OF THE Royal Air Force's new plane, the Hurricane, was tested for the first time in 1935, with full production by its manufacturers, Hawker Aircraft, expected by 1937. The Hurricane, a single-seater fighter, was the first RAF plane to fly over 300 miles per hour.

The building of the Hurricane was one part of a major attempt to increase the Royal Air Force. The British government was thinking mainly in terms of defending Britain, not attacking overseas. By 1935, it was accepted that the German bomber posed the greatest threat to Britain's defences.

Other firsts and records of 1935

THE WORLD'S FIRST parking meter was installed in Oklahoma City in the USA.

The London Underground was being developed in the 1930s and new stations were being built. When Leicester Square Station was opened in May, it boasted the world's longest escalator.

The fastest crossing of the Atlantic was achieved this year, by the French liner *Normandie* on its maiden voyage. It took four days and three hours.

A new altitude record for a balloon of 74,000 feet (22,555 metres) was set in the USA by Orvil Anderson and Andrew Stevens.

Sir Malcolm again . . . and again

SIR MALCOLM CAMPBELL had done it again, twice. Firstly, in March, he set a new land speed record at Daytona Beach of over 276 miles per hour. Then in September he became the first man to travel over 300 miles per hour on land at Bonneville Salt Flats in Utah.

Sir Malcolm Campbell stands beside his record-breaking car, Bluebird. In the car is his son Donald who later became a speed record breaker himself.

1936

Civil war

Popular Front wins elections

DESPITE SEVERAL YEARS of unrest, Spain in 1936 was still a democracy. In February there were new elections.

On the right, the Catholics and Monarchists campaigned together. On the left, Socialists and Communists, with the support of some Republicans, campaigned together under the banner of a Popular Front. A smaller group of moderate Republicans formed a Centre Party between these two.

After six weeks of campaigning voting took place on 16 February. Never in Spanish history had so many voted. The result was a victory for the Popular Front. It received 4,700,000 votes, the right 4,000,000 and the centre only 450,000. The Popular Front gained 257 out of 473 seats in the Cortes, a majority.

The victory of the left was, however, followed not by calm but by increased disorder. Many peasants started seizing land for themselves. In the cities Socialists talked of the victory of the Popular Front as the first step towards a total revolution. In the streets battles broke out between young supporters of both right and left.

Uprising of the army

BY JULY the Spanish army had had enough. It believed that Spain was falling into chaos and that it was its duty to rescue it. Plans were made for the army to rise up against the Republican Popular Front government and seize power.

The uprising began in Spanish Morocco on 17 July where troops seized control of the major cities. By the next day the uprising was under way on mainland Spain. Much of the south and west of Spain fell to the rebels. However, in Madrid the uprising failed and the government of the Popular Front remained in power and determined to resist the army. In Barcelona and other big industrial cities workers and loyal troops helped defeat the uprisings. In the north Catalonia and the Basque country stood firm against it. The navy also remained loyal, its sailors killing officers who tried to seize the ships in support of the army.

Within a few days it was clear that the army had failed to seize control, but it did hold rich wheat-growing areas of Spain and was prepared to fight on. The Civil War was under way. By October the Nationalists had a strong leader, Francisco Franco, an army general who proclaimed himself head of state. He was a dedicated soldier, able to bring together the nationalist groups into an effective fighting force.

Refugees from the Spanish Civil War trudge through the countryside in search of safety.

in Spain

Foreigners intervene

THE CIVIL WAR might have ended sooner and with far less bloodshed if foreign countries had not become so involved. The Nationalists appealed to Germany and Italy and both sent help. German planes were vital in helping General Franco, who had taken command in Morocco, to fly 20,000 of his troops over to mainland Spain. Once these troops had landed they were used to march up from the south of Spain to link up with the western areas of the country already held by the Nationalists. The Portuguese also helped the Nationalists.

The Republican government appealed for help to France but the French government, after sending some planes, decided it could not risk supporting either side. The British government also stood clear of the conflict.

The most practical help the Republicans received was from the Soviet Union. Its first shipment of arms arrived in October comprising 100 tanks, 50 fighter planes and food and medical supplies. This support helped the Republicans to defend Madrid when it came under siege from the Nationalists later in the year.

For many throughout the world, the Spanish Civil War represented a struggle between good and evil, between Fascism and Communism, between the right and the left. About 40,000 foreigners came to Spain as individuals to support the Republic, 10,000 from France, 5000 from Germany and Austria, 5000 from Poland and about 2500 from Britain.

Civilians in Malaga (southern Spain) salute the Nationalist troops who have taken over their province. Note that the salute is the same as used by Fascists in other parts of Europe.

Both sides use terror

It is necessary to create an atmosphere of terror. We have to create this impression of mastery . . . Anyone who is overtly or secretly a supporter of the Republicans must be shot.

These were the words of General Mola, one of the leaders of the uprising.

Both sides in the Spanish Civil War used terror against their enemies in the areas they controlled. In the Republican areas, killer gangs searched out the Catholic clergy – some 4500 priests were killed. In Ronda, a town in southern Spain, over 500 Nationalists were thrown down the deep gorge that divided the town.

The Nationalists killed some 50,000 Republicans in the first six months of the war. The most tragic death was that of the great Spanish poet, Lorca, killed in Grenada in August.

Civil War – the two sides

THE BATTLE LINES for a Civil War in Spain had developed over the previous five years. On the one side there were the traditional and conservative forces in Spanish society: the army; the Catholic Church; those who still supported the monarchy; the big land-owners and businessmen. The army, in particular, saw itself as the guardian of the old Spain. Together these groups of the *right* were known as the Nationalists. Increasingly, many of their supporters looked to Italian fascism and German Nazism as models to follow.

On the other side there were the forces of the *left*, eager for change: workers; landless peasants; national groups such as the Basques and Catalans who resented rule from Madrid. They were a mixed group; moderate middle-class Republicans, suspicious of the power of the Church and army, trade unionists, socialists and a small Communist Party which looked to Russia for support. There were also the anarchists, strong among the poor, who resented any kind of state authority.

Hitler moves troops into the Rhineland

ALTHOUGH THE RHINELAND, the area along the German border with France, Holland and Belgium, was part of Germany, the Germans had been forbidden by the Treaty of Versailles to keep any troops or fortifications there. Hitler was determined to change this.

By March he was ready to move. He knew the French government, the one most likely to resist him, was weak and on bad terms with the British. The Italians, who had opposed him at Stresa a year before, were tied up in Abyssinia and hardly on good terms with Britain and France. He felt he could get away with it.

The German troops moved in on 7 March, a Saturday. They had orders to retreat if the French armies retaliated.

They never did. The French generals thought they were too weak to fight back. The French government asked the British what they thought but received no support. Within a few days the German troops were firmly entrenched and fortifications were being rebuilt along the French border.

League of Nations discredited

THE LEAGUE had briefly discussed cutting off oil exports to Italy in early 1936 but nothing had been agreed. Sanctions might well have proved successful. Mussolini himself admitted that a ban on oil might have stopped the war in Abyssinia within a week.

Soon it was all too late. Abyssinia had fallen. Shortly afterwards all sanctions against Italy were called off. The League had failed and no one took it seriously again.

Edward VIII abdicates

'AFTER I AM DEAD, the boy will ruin himself in twelve months.' So had predicted King George V who died in January. His eldest son, Edward, was 41 but unmarried. For some time he had been involved with an American, Mrs Wallis Simpson, who was shortly to be divorced for the second time.

The new King's relationship was widely known and talked about in London high society and also overseas, but the British press kept silent about it until December. Then suddenly it became public, and the King insisted he wanted to marry Mrs Simpson, causing a major crisis.

The Prime Minister, backed by the Archbishop of Canterbury and the Prime Ministers of the Dominions, made it clear that they would never accept Mrs Simpson as Queen. The King refused to give way and on 11 December he abdicated, leaving for France the next day to join his bride to be.

It was the first abdication of a British monarch since 1399. Edward's brother, until then the Duke of York, succeeded him as King George VI.

A British newspaper headlines the news of the German reoccupation of the Rhineland. Note also the story about a possible air pact between Britain and Germany, a sign that Britain was not seriously thinking of confronting Germany.

The former King Edward VIII, with his bride, Wallis Simpson. After their marriage on 3 June they became the Duke and Duchess of Windsor.

Roosevelt re-elected

ROOSEVELT SWEPT to a stunning victory in the US presidential election of 1936. He lost only two states, Maine and Vermont. Although unemployment still remained high, at nearly 17 per cent in 1936, and there was still appalling misery in the farmlands of the Great Plains where drought had ruined thousands of farmers, Roosevelt remained a centre of hope for millions. He received between 5000 and 8000 letters a day and as a result of his 'Fireside Chats', made over the radio, most Americans felt he really cared about their problems. Above all, in an age of dictators, he had shown that democracy could still work.

'Shoot the mad dogs'

SINISTER NEW DEVELOPMENTS took place in the Soviet Union this year with the first of a series of public 'show trials'. The 16 defendants, senior members of the Communist Party, had mostly been Stalin's rivals for power in the 1920s. They were accused of being in league with Leon Trotsky, the most gifted of Stalin's rivals, who had been forced into exile in 1929 and who was now in Norway. They were also accused of being involved in the murder of Kirov and of plotting the murder of Stalin and other Soviet leaders.

Astonishingly enough, all the accused except one confessed to the charges. No other evidence was offered. 'Shoot the mad dogs' shouted the Chief Prosecutor, Andrei Vyshinsky, at the end of the trial. All 16 were shot the next day.

Italian Empire proclaimed

THE ITALIAN CONQUEST of Abyssinia was finally declared complete in May after the fall of the capital, Addis Ababa. Mussolini proudly proclaimed that Italy now had its own empire. In fact, large areas of the country had not yet been subdued.

The war had cost Italy 5000 lives (most of them troops from its African colonies) and it would take three years of the military budget to make up the equipment lost. Some estimates put the number of Ethiopians killed as high as 500,000.

Italy had successfully defied the League of Nations but was now isolated in Europe. Only Germany appeared a possible ally and during 1936 the two countries began to draw closer together.

Mao Zedong joins forces with Chiang Kaishek

EVER SINCE THE END of the famous Long March in 1935, the Chinese Communists under Mao Zedong, based in the northern province of Shensi, had continued to harass the government forces of Chiang Kaishek, the Nationalist ruler of China. Chiang was using Manchurian troops to try to suppress them, but these troops were far more interested in fighting the Japanese who had overrun their homeland. In December Chiang visited these troops only to be kidnapped by them. He was forced to make peace with the Communists and put all his energies into fighting the Japanese who now seemed poised for another attack on China.

Gone with the Wind – best seller of 1936

AN EPIC NOVEL from the USA, *Gone with the Wind*, was the best seller of 1936. *Gone with the Wind* tells the story of Scarlett O'Hara, the beautiful daughter of a southern landowning family in the USA and is set in the Civil War of 1861 to 1865. Its author, Margaret Mitchell, took ten years to write it, and it was an immediate success, selling a million copies in six months. The film rights were quickly snapped up and the search was on to find an actress to play Scarlett.

Popular films of 1936

Charlie Chaplin was in the film news again with *Modern Times*, a film about the tyranny of the machine over the ordinary man.

Howard Hawks had already made his name as director of *Scarface*. Now in *Road to Glory* he used a story of the horrors of trench warfare in the First World War to spread a strong anti-war message.

On a more romantic note, *Showboat* was the story of life and love aboard an oldtime Mississippi showboat

---

Lorca killed in Spain

THE GREAT SPANISH POET and dramatist, Federico Garcia Lorca, died in 1936, killed by the Nationalists at the beginning of the Spanish Civil War. He was just 37. Lorca's most famous plays were *Blood Wedding* and *Yerma*. His work was inspired by the deep emotions and passions he found among the Spanish people. Lorca had his own group of actors whom he took around the villages of Spain to perform his plays.

Charlie Chaplin in one of his best known films of the 1930s, Modern Times. *The film warned of how modern factory life could crush the spirit of the individual.*

Surrealist art shocks many

OVER 20,000 PEOPLE flocked to the International Surrealist Exhibition held at the New Burlington Galleries in London this June. Among the exhibits was the artist Salvador Dali who appeared, with two Irish wolfhounds, in a diving suit with a motor-car radiator cap on the top.

Not everyone appreciated the exhibition.

Decadence and unhealthiness of mind and body, the unleashing of low and abnormal instincts, a total lack of reason and balance, a distasteful revelation of subconscious thoughts and desires . . . these words are not too strong for some exhibits . . . the authorities should now step into the galleries and ruthlessly tear several pictures from the walls, pictures certainly unfit for the eyes of the public at large.
The *Daily Mail*

Jesse Owens stuns the Germans

THE BRILLIANT AMERICAN athlete Jesse Owens exploded the Nazi theory that blacks were inferior when he won four gold medals at the Olympic Games held in Berlin, the capital of Hitler's Germany. Germany had been awarded the 1936 Games before Hitler came to power, but the Nazis were determined to exploit the Games for all they were worth. Every effort was made to portray Germany as a tolerant and friendly state. Violence against Jews was brought under control but renewed as soon as the thousands of foreign visitors had gone home.

Owens' gold medals were for the 100 metres and 200 metres, the Long Jump and 400 metre relay.

Perry wins Wimbledon

FRED PERRY, Britain's tennis star, won Wimbledon for the third time in a row this year. He later crossed the Atlantic to become the first foreigner to win the US championship.

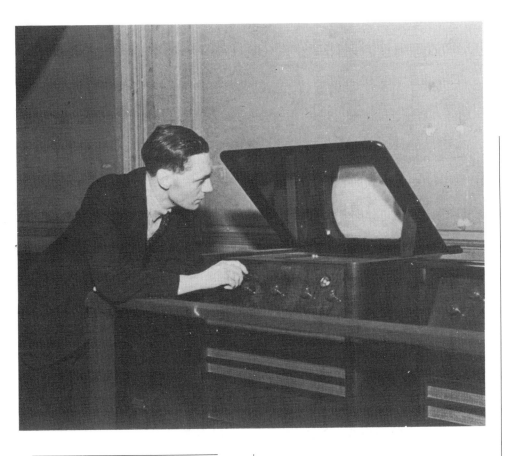

Electron microscope goes into production

THE ELECTRON MICROSCOPE had been invented by the German electrical engineer, Ernst Ruska, in 1933. He realized that waves transmitted by electrons were much shorter than those of normal light and thus could allow objects to be seen in far greater detail when magnified. By 1934 electron microscopes were producing better pictures than the existing optical microscopes but the heat of the electrons tended to damage whatever was being looked at. This problem took some time to overcome but by 1936 the first electron microscopes were in production.

Television service operating

THERE MAY HAVE BEEN only 280 television sets in Britain by the end of 1936, but a television service was operating. Transmitting from a corner of Alexandra Palace in North London, the service began in August when a picture was sent from the Palace to fascinated crowds visiting the Radio Show at Olympia. A singer, Helen McKay, greeted them with a song, 'Here's looking at you, From out of the blue'.

The BBC had experimented with both John Logie Baird's and the EMI-Marconi team's systems but quickly found the electronic scanning of the EMI system much superior and it was soon adopted.

Queen Mary beats record

THE ATLANTIC was crossed in under four days for the first time in August when the British liner the *Queen Mary* achieved a crossing in three days, 23 hours and 57 minutes.

The Atlantic was also crossed for the first time from Europe in an aircraft piloted by a woman on her own, when the 33-year-old British pilot, Beryl Markham, made the crossing in early September.

Girl with the golden voice

FOR THE FIRST TIME in Britain it was possible to ring up to find the time. Miss Jane Cain, a telephonist from Croydon, was selected to make the recording and quickly became known as the 'Girl with the Golden Voice'. Nearly a quarter of a million calls were made to hear her voice, or find out the time, in the week the service began.

Radar spreads along the coast

FOLLOWING THE SUCCESSFUL testing of radar in 1935 radar masts were erected near Dover, Canterbury, Southend and Colchester. The aim was to have the entire eastern and southern coasts of Britain covered by radar by 1939.

German bombers hit Guernica

ON MONDAY 26 APRIL at 4.30 pm the bells of the small Basque town of Guernica rang out in warning of an air raid. The town was now only ten miles from the front of the Spanish Civil War and Nationalist forces were moving rapidly towards it. It was crowded with refugees and the retreating soldiers of the Republican armies. There were no air defences.

Forty-three planes of the German *Luftwaffe*'s Condor Squadron, both fighters and bombers, were soon overhead dropping bombs. About 45,000 kilograms of incendiaries, high explosive and shrapnel bombs were dropped, and those fleeing from the town were machine-gunned by the fighters. Over 70 per cent of the town was destroyed and at least 100 died.

When the Nationalist troops took the town three days later, they tried to conceal the truth about the raid by claiming that the Basques had set fire to the town themselves.

war fever

Japanese bomb China

IN AUGUST the Japanese, already firmly in control in the northern Chinese province of Manchuria, struck southwards mounting heavy bombing raids on major Chinese towns. In the great trading port of Shanghai over 2000 civilians died in bombing raids, 1000 of them in an amusement park which came under attack. In Chiang Kai-shek's capital, Nanking, 200 were reported dead in raids there.

By December both Shanghai and Nanking had been captured and large areas of China had fallen under Japanese control.

When war resumed in the Far East the coastal towns of China were brutally bombed into submission.

Gas masks issued

THE GREATEST FEAR in the late 1930s was that the bombs dropped would not contain explosives but poison gas, as had been used in the First World War. At least one popular novel started with a picture of London standing unharmed but with all the inhabitants killed by gas. So by 1937 preparations were in hand to provide gas masks for all who needed them. Although gas attacks were never made, gas masks became a part of everyday life in big cities such as London.

For the first time civilians throughout Europe were being issued with gas masks because of fears that gas bombs would be dropped on towns. This picture is of a girl in Czechoslovakia.

Failure to ban bombing

EVER SINCE the First World War statesmen had been aware that mass bombing would be a major threat in the warfare of the future. There had been endless discussions on how to limit bombing to military targets or just to areas where fighting was actually taking place, with a ban on bombing in other areas. All the discussions came to nothing. Thus by the late 1930s there were no agreed restrictions on the use of explosives in time of war. There had, however, been an agreement made at Geneva in 1925 that poison gas would not be used in war. No one knew whether the promise not to use gas would be honoured.

600,000 would die in 60 days

IN BRITAIN, FRANCE and other countries, people were at last waking up to what the next war might really be like. The British Cabinet was warned that if war broke out with Germany, Britain could expect a German air attack spread over 60 days which would leave 600,000 dead and 1,200,000 injured. The House of Commons, meanwhile, passed the first measures allowing air raid shelters to be constructed in major cities.

At the same time the BBC was suddenly becoming aware of the fact that its main control room, a vital centre for sending out information at time of war, had been placed on the top floor of Broadcasting House, and was thus immediately vulnerable to attack.

George VI crowned

WITH THE ABDICATION of Edward VIII in 1936, his younger brother George succeeded him as King. National loyalty remained high throughout the thirties and centred on the Royal Family.

Faith in the monarchy had taken a knock with Edward's decision to marry the divorcee Wallis Simpson and his consequent clash with the government. This faith was restored however by George VI and his immensely popular Queen, Elizabeth (now the Queen Mother). His Coronation in May this year provided the focus for a celebration of British traditions and values which had survived the miseries of unemployment and poverty. Festive street parties took place in local communities throughout the country.

More Soviet show trials

THERE WERE TWO MORE major 'show trials' in the Soviet Union in 1937. In January another group of leading party members was accused of being in league with Trotsky and of attempting to wreck industry. Thirteen of the 17 accused were shot and the others were imprisoned. In June a group of eight generals was accused of a conspiracy against Stalin. Their trial lasted only an hour before they too were convicted and shot.

Meanwhile, thousands upon thousands of ordinary citizens were being picked up and sent off to the labour camps of the Gulag. Everyone was urged to watch out for enemies of the people, as the following extract from the Communist Party newspaper *Pravda* shows.

Mussolini meets Hitler

BENITO MUSSOLINI, the Fascist leader of Italy, paid his first visit to Hitler's Germany in September. Although he would not admit it publicly, Mussolini was much impressed by the enormous military parades that were laid on for him. From now on, he announced, Italy and Germany would march together to spread Fascism and fight Communism. He let Hitler know that he would no longer oppose a German take-over of Austria. In November Mussolini was persuaded by Hitler to join the anti-Communist pact which Germany and Japan had made in November 1936.

Mussolini paid his first visit to Hitler's Germany in September, and a massive military parade was laid on for him.

Big blow for the New Deal

IN THE USA, Roosevelt's second term of office was shadowed by conflicts with the Supreme Court, which had the power to condemn laws passed by federal government as unconstitutional. It used this power against many of Roosevelt's New Deal initiatives including major policies such as higher wages, better working conditions and support for trade unionism. In 1937, with another plunge in the American economy, Roosevelt was pressed by advisers into cutting public spending, with the result that unemployment had risen by 2 million at the end of the year.

It is the duty of the Soviet citizen to view his surroundings critically and to know well the people with whom he works or is friendly. The honest Soviet citizen must not only beware of spies, he must actively aid in the repudiation of the undermining activity of agents of foreign intelligence services . . . someone in a neighbouring apartment may have peculiar visitors and carry on anti-Soviet conversations with them. That should be reported to the organs of State security. Yet some people think differently. They do not like to 'tell on' a neighbour. This false conception of 'telling on' must be done away with once and for all.
Pravda, 30 July.

New British Prime Minister

FOLLOWING THE RETIREMENT of Stanley Baldwin, the Chancellor of the Exchequer, Neville Chamberlain, became Prime Minister. Chamberlain had the reputation of being a good and careful administrator but had very little experience of foreign affairs. He believed, however, that, with good sense and co-operation between world leaders, peace in Europe could be maintained. War, he felt, must be avoided at almost any cost, as another conflict on the scale of the First World War would destroy the countries which fought it. His policy, known as appeasement, was to listen to the grievances of Hitler and to see how far he could meet them.

Plan to divide Palestine

PALESTINE was in the news after publication of the British Government's plan, the result of a commission headed by Lord Peel, to share the territory between the Jews and Arabs. The British had taken control of Palestine after the First World War and had agreed that Jews might return to

the area, their ancient homeland. By 1936 there were 400,000 Jews living there, as against a million Arab Palestinians who deeply resented what was happening. Following riots in 1936, the Peel Commission saw the only solution as to split the territory between the two groups. The Arabs, however, would never accept what would be the loss of part of their own homeland while many Jews wanted Palestine to be all-Jewish.

Hitler plans war

ON 5 NOVEMBER Hitler had a secret meeting with the chiefs of his armed forces and his foreign minister, Baron von Neurath. He told them that Germany must now plan for war. Other nations were rearming and if Germany did not take action soon, it would have lost its advantage. The first target must be Czechoslovakia, so that Germany would be strong in the east in case of attack in the future from France in the west.

In December the German army planners adopted the plan of war known as Operation Green which involved a massive attack on Czechoslovakia. The plan was still a secret to Germany's neighbours.

Sport and the Arts

Some day my prince will come

SO SANG SNOW WHITE in Walt Disney's *Snow White and the Seven Dwarfs*, one of the big hits of 1937. It was Walt Disney's first full-length feature and took three years and 2 million drawings to complete.

On a more serious note was the French director, Jean Renoir's, *La Grande Illusion*. Set in a German prison camp, the film examines the collapse of the old Europe and the futility of war. It calls for an end to national and class hatreds. With brilliant acting and photography, it has lasted as one of the most important films of the 1930s.

The Road to Wigan Pier

ONE OF THE MOST TALKED about books of the year in Britain was *The Road to Wigan Pier* by George Orwell. It described Orwell's visit in 1936 to the north of England where he explored the life of the working class, visiting their homes, venturing down a coal mine and so on. The second part of the book contained his ideas for the building of a stronger socialist movement in Britain, one which would appeal to the mass of ordinary people. *The Road to Wigan Pier* was published by the Left Book Club, a club which had been founded the year before by the publisher, Victor Gollancz, to attack the evils of Fascism and Nazism.

Margot Fonteyn reaches stardom

FOR THE FIRST TIME England had produced a ballet dancer of international stature. The 17-year-old Margot Fonteyn took over the lead in the ballet *Giselle* at Sadlers Wells and scored an immediate triumph.

Guernica dominates Paris Exhibition

THE MAJOR PAINTING of 1937 was *Guernica* by Pablo Picasso. It was commissioned by the Republican government of Spain to form part of the Spanish Pavilion at the World Fair held in Paris. *Guernica*, a huge painting, nearly eight metres long, depicts the horror of the bombing of the Basque town Guernica, which had taken place in April. A soldier lies dead while women scream in the aftermath of the bombing.

Picasso's Guernica *expresses the horrors of the Spanish Civil War.*

'Brown Bomber' storms to title

THE AMERICAN BOXER Joe Louis, also known as the 'Brown Bomber', became world heavyweight boxing champion on 22 June. He knocked out the previous champion, James Braddock, in eight rounds in Chicago. Joe Louis went on to hold his title for nearly 12 years, the longest reign of any boxing world champion in history.

Hindenburg crashes

ON 6 MAY the German airship, *Hindenburg*, crashed in New Jersey when coming in to land after crossing the Atlantic. Thirty-three passengers and crew died.

This latest disaster brought the end of the age of the airship. Both of the largest US airships, the *Akron* and the *Macon*, had also crashed and it was clear that no one could guarantee the safety of airships.

In 1936 a Short flying boat (a long distance aircraft, capable of landing on water) had flown from Southampton in England to Sydney in Australia with 23 passengers in nine and a half days. By 1937 trial mail flights were being made across the Atlantic. Soon aircraft would be able to fly safely and regularly between continents and there would no longer be a need to use airships for long distance travel.

First nylon stockings being made

THE DEVELOPMENT of new types of fibres in the early 1930s was now at last bearing fruit. In 1937 the Du Pont Company in the USA was able to make nylon stockings for the first time, although they were not yet put on sale to the general public.

Amelia Earhart lost

THE AMERICAN WOMAN AVIATOR, Amelia Earhart, famous for her solo crossing of the Atlantic in 1932, and the first successful flight from Hawaii to the USA in 1935, disappeared on a flight round the world in July. She was two-thirds of the way round when her plane is believed to have crashed in the middle of the Pacific Ocean.

The crash of the Hindenburg *in May saw the end of the airships.*

Lord Rutherford dies

ONE OF THE GREATEST SCIENTISTS of the twentieth century, Ernest Rutherford, died in October. Born in New Zealand, he came to Cambridge on a scholarship in 1893. His early work was on radio-activity, much of it carried out in Canada. In 1919 he was appointed Professor of Experimental Physics at Cambridge and at the Cavendish Laboratory he collected a group of brilliant young scientists around him, including those who split the atom for the first time. Rutherford was buried in Westminster Abbey.

World's longest suspension bridge opens

THE GOLDEN GATE BRIDGE, spanning the Golden Gate, the entrance to San Francisco, was finally completed in 1937. It was the world's longest suspension bridge with a main span of 4200 feet (1280 metres). Its foundations were specially constructed so as to be earthquake proof. The fast-flowing tides and the frequent storms of the area made its completion an outstanding feat of engineering.

1938

The Czech

Hitler moves eastwards

HITLER DRAMATICALLY expanded the borders of Germany to the east this year. In March, after sending German troops there, he announced union, or *Anschluss*, with Austria, the land of his birth. The union was greeted with enthusiasm by the majority of the Austrian people. Since the break-up of the Austrian Empire in 1918, Austria had been a small and impoverished country and the Austrians, many of whom were Nazi supporters, now hoped for a better future within the new Germany.

Hitler's next target was the German-speaking people of Czechoslovakia. The Sudeten Germans, as they were called, lived along the Czech borders, separated from Germany by a mountain range. Hitler claimed that they were being badly treated by the Czechs and had the right to be joined to Germany if they wished. If they and this range were joined to Germany, however, the rest of Czechoslovakia and the lands further east would lie open to German power. By September Hitler was threatening immediate action, even war, if he did not get his way.

German police arrive in newly occupied Austria, Hitler's birthplace, now united with Germany.

Munich agreement made

NEVILLE CHAMBERLAIN, Prime Minister of Britain, was determined to avoid war over Czechoslovakia. 'How horrible, fantastic, incredible it is', he told the British people, as tension grew in September, 'that we should be digging trenches and trying on gas masks here because of a quarrel in a far-away country between people of whom we know nothing'. In a desperate bid to save the peace Chamberlain paid three visits to Hitler. The third was held in Munich on 29 September when Germany and its ally, Italy, agreed with Britain and France that the Sudetenland with its 3 million Germans should indeed be handed over to Germany.

Chamberlain flew home in triumph carrying a piece of paper he and Hitler had signed which proclaimed their intention never to go to war again. Only a few in Britain worried about Czechoslovakia which had been bullied into giving up territory and now lay open to further German expansion.

problem

'It is peace for our time', proclaimed Neville Chamberlain on his return from Munich in September. Less than a year later the Second World War had begun.

Why did Chamberlain do it?

CHAMBERLAIN was determined to keep Britain out of war. He knew the British people, haunted by the horrors of the First World War, did not want it. He knew too that Britain was threatened by the growing power of Japan in the east and could not afford to be on bad terms with Germany as well. His concern this year was to keep peace at any price, and the vast majority of the population enthusiastically supported him in this.

However, there was more to it than that. Chamberlain believed that he had a special relationship with Hitler, and that he and Hitler could come to binding agreements which would provide a fair solution to Germany's grievances. He completely failed to realize that Hitler had no intention of keeping agreements and was ruthlessly set on expansion.

Churchill condemns Munich agreement

IN THE DEBATE on the Munich agreement which took place in the British House of Commons in the first week of October, Winston Churchill, a member of Chamberlain's own party but his strongest critic, denounced the betrayal of Czechoslovakia:

All is over. Silent, mournful, abandoned, broken, Czechoslovakia recedes into the darkness. You will find that in a period of time which may be measured by years, but may be measured by months, Czechoslovakia will be engulfed by the Nazi regime . . . . Our people should know that we have sustained a defeat without a war, the consequences of which will travel far with us along our road; they should know that we have passed an awful milestone in our history, when the whole equilibrium of Europe has been deranged, and that the terrible words have for the time being been pronounced against the Western democracies: 'Thou art weighed in the balance and found wanting'.

Benes resigns

The sacrifices demanded from us were immeasurably great and immeasurably unjust. This the nation will never forget, even though they have borne these sacrifices quietly.

President Benes, addressing the Czech nation, on 30 September, shortly before resigning and going into exile.

French follow British example

UNLIKE THE BRITISH, the French had a treaty with Czechoslovakia, one which stated that they would come to its help if it were attacked. However, the French government, under the leadership of Prime Minister Deladier, had no will to save the Czech borders. France was economically weak, never having recovered fully from the Depression, and politically unstable. The French were content simply to follow the line established by Neville Chamberlain of accepting Hitler's demands.

There was a difference. Chamberlain thought he had achieved a triumph for Britain. Deladier knew he had brought disaster to France. His betrayal of Czechoslovakia had lost France her only firm European ally. 'Les cons', ('the fools'), he said of the crowd which greeted him. He knew just how weak France really was.

World News

Munich crisis tests British nerves

THE BRITISH PUBLIC faced the first real test of air raid precautions during the Munich crisis. It was the common belief that war, if it came, would start with attacks from the air, possibly involving the use of gas. At the height of the crisis trenches were dug in the public parks in London and 44 anti-aircraft guns were positioned round the capital. Air raid warning sirens were broadcast over the BBC so that everyone would know how they sounded, and 38 million gas masks were sent to distribution centres round Britain. Arrangements were made to evacuate all children from large cities. In fact, this 'trial run' showed how much still needed to be done and after the crisis was over the Government at last got down to serious planning.

The Home Office announces that the designing of gas masks for babies has been difficult but this has been surmounted and production is now in hand; in the meantime a good measure of protection can be afforded by wrapping the baby completely in a blanket when it could with safety be carried through gas to the nearest gas-proof shelter.
Government announcement, 1938.

A distressed woman brought her bowl of goldfish with her when she went to be fitted for a gas mask. How could they be protected. 'They'll be all right, ma'am,' a friendly air raid warden reassured her, 'just put them in your mask along with you.'

Palestine crisis

BY 1938 THE BRITISH were fighting what amounted to a small war in Palestine. The Arab population, infuriated at continued Jewish immigration, was in open revolt. Armed groups roamed the countryside and the British enforced a military occupation. Nearly 2000 people died during the year. In 1939 the British finally agreed that Jewish immigration would have to be limited

Soviet defence budget rises

STALIN'S PURGES continued through 1938. By the end of the year about 35,000 officers had been expelled from the army, including 90 per cent of the generals. However, by the end of the year Stalin called an end to the purges. The continual removal of key experts was leading to chaos. After years of impressive growth, iron and steel production actually fell during 1938.

Stalin now realized that the Soviet Union was surrounded by danger. Japan was expanding in the east. In the west Britain and France with whom Stalin had hoped to make alliances had signed away the Czech borders at Munich and thus made the Soviet Union more vulnerable to attack from Germany. In the new Five Year Plan, starting this year, Stalin poured new resources into defence.

Nationalists tighten grip

THE NATIONALISTS, firmly united under General Franco, moved towards victory in the Spanish Civil War. The different Republican groups were quarrelling among themselves and during the year their supplies from Russia began to dry up. Franco was still receiving help from Germany and Italy. In March he broke through to the Mediterranean coast splitting the Republican-held areas. The Republicans fought back with a major attack along the River Ebro but they were soon exhausted and by the end of the year they were in retreat.

to a total of 75,000 over five years. The Jews, faced with renewed persecution in Germany and desperate for a safe home, felt betrayed.

Japanese bombing continues. This destruction is in Shanghai. By this time enormous areas of Northern China were under Japanese control.

On Krystallnacht, *the Night of the Broken Glass, Jewish businesses were ransacked. Many Germans, including the woman in this picture, appeared to support the violence.*

Japan overruns northern China

THE JAPANESE CONTINUED to make major advances into northern China and by the middle of the year they controlled all the main railway lines and major cities of the north. The capital, Nanking, had fallen at the end of 1937. The new capital, Han-k'ou, 400 miles further inland fell in October. In the same month another important port, Canton, in the south, fell almost without resistance. The Chinese government had to retreat further inland finally making its base at Chungking behind a protective range of mountains.

Krystallnacht in Germany

FOLLOWING THE SHOOTING of a German official at the Paris Embassy by a Polish Jew, the German Propaganda Minister, Josef Goebbels, organized a violent attack on the Jewish community in November. In the 'Night of the Broken Glass' (*Krystallnacht*) 90 died and thousands of Jewish homes, businesses and synagogues were smashed up by gangs of stormtroopers. Thirty-five thousand Jews were taken to concentration camps.

Even before *Krystallnacht* there had been renewed pressure on Jews this year. They had been excluded from most of the professions and many of their businesses had been taken over by German firms.

Hurricane in America

IN SEPTEMBER one of the worst hurricanes in American history hit the prosperous coastline of Long Island and New England. The weather forecasters completely failed to predict its strength as it roared across the Atlantic. The coast guard was not even alerted. The impact of the first storm wave which hit the coast was registered in Alaska several thousand miles away. Thirty-room mansions in the prosperous Long Island summer resorts disintegrated and 63,000 people were made homeless. Some 700 people died and it was estimated that if the hurricane had hit the coast during the holiday season over 6000 would have been killed.

Sport and the Arts

Americans set new tennis records

THE AMERICAN TENNIS PLAYER Don Budge became the first man ever to hold all four major tennis championships, the US, Wimbledon, Australian and French, at once, when he won the final one of the four, the French championship. Budge had won the men's singles, men's doubles and mixed doubles at Wimbledon both in 1937 and again in 1938. Another American, Helen Moody, won her eighth Wimbledon women's singles championship in 1938, a record. She had won previously in 1927, 1928, 1929, 1930, 1932, 1933 and 1935.

New British sculptors

BRITISH ARTISTS HAD on the whole been slow to fall in with the experimental movements led by Picasso, Braque, Duchamp, Klee and others on the Continent and in the USA. However, by the late thirties several new names had emerged who could hold their own with the best. Important new works appeared in 1938 by sculptors Henry Moore (born 1898) and Barbara Hepworth (born 1903). Moore's *Reclining Figure* is typical of his sensuous combination of abstract and representational forms, the result of his great feeling for the natural qualities of his stone materials. Hepworth's *Forms in Échelon* is also typical of the artist's work, a more abstract approach than Moore's, but still close to human scale and proportions.

Gamblers go for football pools

GAMBLING was a widespread occupation for all classes in the Britain of the 1930s. The football pools were the most popular with an estimated 10 million people sending in weekly coupons by 1938, bringing total business of some 10 to 15 million letters a week for the Post Office. The big firms, Vernons and Littlewoods, employed hundreds of staff and spent some £20,000 a week on newspaper advertising.

Betting on greyhounds followed close behind. In one greyhound stadium the operators could deal with 27,000 bets a minute. Surveys on gambling showed that most people bet small amounts weekly and used considerable skill in picking out likely winners.

Year of the epics

THIS YEAR SAW the production of two major film epics. From Germany, Leni Riefenstahl, director of *Triumph of the Will*, now produced her *Olympic Games*, a glorification of human achievement in sport. From Russia, the film *Alexander Nevsky*, directed by Sergei Eisenstein, told the story of a thirteenth-century Russian leader fighting off invasion from the West. It was clearly aimed at warning Russian audiences of the threat from Nazi Germany.

'End of the world' panic

AN EXTRAORDINARY wave of hysteria swept the USA on 30 October, when a radio play which included an invasion from Mars was believed by thousands of listeners to be a real news broadcast. The play, a dramatization by the actor Orson Welles of H.G. Wells novel, *The War of the Worlds*, brought sobbing crowds into the streets and led to radio and police switchboards being jammed with panic calls.

New English cricket record

THE ENGLISH CRICKET TEAM set an unbeaten record in the Fifth Test against Australia when they scored 903 runs for seven. This was the highest score ever reached in England, although an Australian team had scored 1107 runs in Melbourne in 1926. Len Hutton scored 364 runs and the match ended with a victory for England by an innings and 579 runs.

Queen Elizabeth launched

THE *QUEEN ELIZABETH* was the largest passenger ship ever built and weighed 85,016 tonnes. It was 314 metres long and its steam turbine engines generated 168,000 horse power. It was to be launched by the King, George VI, on 27 September but because of the Munich crisis he felt unable to leave London and his Queen, Elizabeth, after whom the ship was named, performed the ceremony.

First Spitfires delivered

A NEW FIGHTER PLANE, the Spitfire, was put into operation with the RAF this year as part of Britain's expansion of its air forces. The Spitfire had a single engine but was one of the fastest military aircraft in the world. It could also carry light bombs. By October 13 Spitfires a month were being produced and there was a separate Spitfire squadron. Hurricanes made up the planes of the other five RAF squadrons. Britain had 1854 aircraft in 1938 compared to 2847 in Germany but Britain was expanding production much faster than Germany.

BBC foreign language broadcasts

IN JANUARY the BBC began to broadcast for the first time in a foreign language. The first foreign broadcasts were in Arabic followed, later in the year, by broadcasts in Spanish and Portuguese. This new service developed into the BBC World Service.

Anderson shelters arrive

AFTER RENEWED DISCUSSION as to how to deal with air raids, the British government decided against building deep shelters. Instead plans were announced for making 400,000 small steel shelters which could be dug into back gardens and which would be made available free of charge for poorer people. The shelters were named after Sir John Anderson, a brilliant civil servant, who had become a Member of Parliament and put in charge of air raid precautions.

First living coelecanth discovered

A TRAWLER fishing off the coast of South Africa had a very strange catch this year. It was a large fish nearly two metres long with powerful jaws and heavy armoured scales. Nothing like it had been seen before.

At last experts identified it. It was a coelecanth, an early form of fish which had originated 350 million years ago but was believed to have been extinct for 70 million years. It had lived deep down near the sea bed completely unknown until this year. The search was now on to find other specimens.

Mallard sets all-time steam record

AN ALL-TIME SPEED RECORD for a steam engine was set on 3 July when the L.N.E.R. 4-6-2 *Mallard* reached 126 miles per hour on a quarter mile stretch between Grantham and Peterborough. The engine suffered severe damage in the run.

Mallard *set the record speed of 126 miles per hour which has never since been broken by a steam train.*

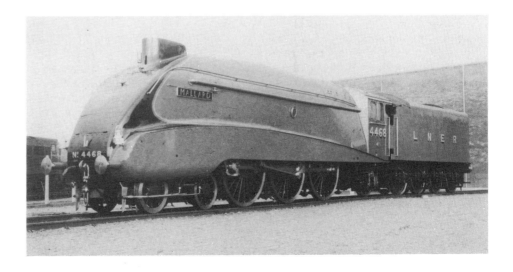

Germany smashes Poland

THE SECOND WORLD WAR finally began on 1 September when German troops and aircraft smashed their way into Poland. The Poles resisted gallantly but they had little modern equipment and were soon in retreat. Worse was to come on 17 September when Soviet troops, under the secret terms of the Nazi-Soviet Pact, swarmed into Poland from the east. By 28 September Warsaw, the Polish capital, had been bombed into surrender and Poland began to experience the horrors of occupation by two dominating and ruthless powers.

Britain and France had both declared war on Germany in support of Poland but were unable to do anything to help the Poles.

The invasion of Poland began when German troops smashed their way through the frontier posts.

Chamberlain makes Polish guarantee

IN MARCH Hitler summoned President Hacha of Czechoslovakia to Germany and forced him to surrender the central areas of Czechoslovakia. German troops quickly moved in, in face of the bitter opposition of the Czechs. Slovakia, in the east of the country, was to become a German protectorate.

The occupation of Czechoslovakia finally brought home to Chamberlain how far he had been misled by Hitler. He now realized that Poland was the next victim on Hitler's list and on 3 March, with French support, he guaranteed that Britain would come to Poland's help if it were attacked.

declared

"WHAT, ME? NO, I NEVER TOUCH GOLDFISH!"

Because of the Nazi-Soviet pact made in August the smaller nations of Eastern Europe were put at the mercy of Germany and the Soviet Union.

Nazi-Soviet pact seals Poland's fate

POLAND'S FATE WAS SEALED by one of the most extraordinary agreements of modern times. The Soviet Union and Nazi Germany had been sworn enemies. After all, the Germans had occupied vast areas of Russia in the First World War. Now, however, they agreed they would not attack each other. Secretly, they went further. The Soviet Union was to be allowed to occupy eastern Poland while Germany was to have the west. In addition,

Germany agreed to stand aside if the Soviet Union took over the small independent Baltic states of Lithuania, Latvia and Estonia.

Both countries benefited from the pact. Hitler now knew he could attack Poland freely. The Soviet Union had bought time to build up its defences in case of a future war with Germany, a war Stalin believed would come sooner or later.

Britain is at War

I am speaking to you from the Cabinet Room at 10, Downing Street. This morning the British Ambassador in Berlin handed the German Government a final note stating that unless we heard from them by 11 o'clock that they were prepared to withdraw their troops from Poland a state of war would exist between us.

I have to tell you now that no such undertaking has been received and consequently this country is at war with Germany.

Neville Chamberlain announcing a state of war, 3 September 1939.

Steps to war

MARCH. HITLER forces President Hacha to surrender central Czechoslovakia to Germany. Slovakia, in the eastern part of the country, becomes a German protectorate.

21 March. Germany forces Lithuania to surrender the disputed city of Memel.

31 March. Chamberlain guarantees to come to the aid of Poland if it is attacked. The French support Britain.

April. Mussolini overruns Albania.

13 April. Britain and France guarantee Romania and Greece.

18 April. Stalin asks Britain and France to make a pact of mutual assistance with him. Discussions lead nowhere.

22 May. Germany makes the so-called Pact of Steel with Italy.

23 August. Germany makes a non-aggression pact with the Soviet Union.

1 September. Hitler invades Poland.

3 September. Britain and France declare war on Germany.

Graf Spee scuttled

ONE OF THE MOST DANGEROUS German surface ships was the pocket-battleship *Graf Spee*. It was fast and heavily armed and was searching out enemy ships in the Atlantic. It was finally cornered by British and New Zealand cruisers and driven into harbour at the River Plate in Uruguay. When it was forced to leave by the Uruguayans the crew was disembarked and the ship sunk. The Captain shot himself. The end of the *Graf Spee* was a great boost to British morale. Britain had already lost one passenger liner, the *Athenia*, and two major warships, the *Courageous* and the *Royal Oak*, to German U-Boats and was in need of good news from the war at sea.

Britain ready for attacks

AS SOON AS WAR broke out everyone in Britain prepared for air raids. All primary school children and mothers with children under five were supposed to leave areas likely to be bombed. In fact, less than half did so but it was a major operation to transport these evacuees to the countryside and find new homes for them. All streetlighting was put out and, at first, cars could not even use their headlamps. Hospitals were set aside for the thousands of casualties it was thought air raids would bring.

However, there were no raids in 1939. More people died from road accidents in unlit streets than from enemy action. This was the period of the 'Phoney War' in Britain, a war which did not seem to be real.

Air raid shelters arrived in London this year. These Anderson shelters were distributed free to poorer London homes. They could be erected by two people.

In the aftermath of the Civil War Spanish refugees fled to France as the Nationalist leader, Franco, declared victory.

Refugees flee from Spain

WITH THE FALL of Barcelona in January and the capture of Madrid in March, the Spanish Civil War ended with the Nationalists victorious and General Franco as new head of state. Some 500,000 Spaniards had died in the conflict. As the Nationalist armies spread into Catalonia in the north, thousands fled as refugees over the French border. The *Manchester Guardian* reported as follows on 30 January:

Fifteen thousand refugees crossed the frontier from Spain into France yesterday and today the flight from Franco continued. Forty-five thousand more are expected to cross the border shortly . . . . Wounded soldiers with their feet swathed in bandages and their arms in plaster casts and steel frames hobbled along; women reached safety carrying heavy suitcases and bundles on their heads; old people and children huddled together in blankets on the station platform. Every particle of food offered to them was ravenously devoured by people who had not eaten for days.

Altogether some 300,000 Spaniards became permanent refugees as a result of the war.

Soviet Union invades Finland

THE SOVIET UNION was desperate to improve the security of its borders, especially around Leningrad in the north. To do this it needed to control parts of Finland. When the Finns refused to give up territory, the Russians attacked. They had assumed that it would be an easy victory but the Finns resisted magnificently. The Finns hoped for outside help and there were British and French plans to bring help. They were all too late. Eventually the Russian armies overcame their opponents and Finland surrendered in March 1940.

USA to remain neutral

WHEN WAR STARTED in Europe in September most Americans believed, or at least hoped, they could stay out of it. Roosevelt publicly supported this ideal but he realized more than most Americans the threat that a German dominated Europe would pose for the USA and the rest of the world.

His first move to help Britain and France came with the 'cash and carry' law of November. From now on any nation could come and buy arms from the USA so long as they paid cash for them and carried them off in their own ships. In practice, it was Britain and France who were able to find the ships to carry off the goods and who, in comparison to Germany now in control of Central Europe, needed them most.

IRA campaign

THE IRA LAUNCHED a campaign of bombing on mainland Britain this year as part of their attempt to drive British forces out of Northern Ireland. They let off 127 bombs, including one in Coventry which killed five people. Other explosions took place at London railway stations and in Piccadilly Circus. The British government introduced anti-terrorist laws which allowed it to make arrests and expel suspects from Britain. The organizer of the IRA campaign, Sean Russell, later sought help from Nazi Germany but without success.

Treasure discovered in Suffolk

AS THE WAR CLOUDS gathered over Europe, archaeologists hurried to complete the excavation of a buried ship found in a mound overlooking the River Deben at Sutton Hoo in Suffolk. The ship was a real sea-going vessel, 25 metres long. In the ship was found the richest treasure ever discovered in Britain, the gold and silver of an early Anglo-Saxon king, whose body was never found. Archaeologists dated the ship burial to the seventh century AD. The treasures came from all over Europe and from even as far as the Middle East.

Yeats is dead

ONE OF THE GREAT English-speaking poets of Ireland, W.B. Yeats, died in January. His haunting poems and plays explore the old traditions of Ireland and its search for a national identity in the years of the struggle for independence. Yeats had a love-hate relationship with Ireland, never feeling its people were worthy of greater traditions in the past. In his later years he looked outside Ireland to Italy and the religious traditions of the East for inspiration. He had been awarded the Nobel Prize for Literature in 1923.

Stagecoach brings the return of the Western

WESTERNS had been popular in the 1920s but few had been made in the 1930s. John Ford's *Stagecoach* marked the start of a new craze for Westerns.

Stagecoach is the story of a group of misfits making a dangerous journey through enemy Indian territory. It is set in the harsh desert plains of Arizona and glorifies the toughness of the individual in a hostile environment.

Other big hits of the year included *Gone with the Wind* and *The Wizard of Oz*, both from the MGM studio. In *Gone with the Wind*, a young English actress, Vivien Leigh, carried off the most sought after role of the year, as the beautiful Scarlett O'Hara, and won an Oscar. Judy Garland was the star of *The Wizard of Oz*. Both films were made in Technicolor, still a very expensive process, but a sign that black and white films would soon be as dated as silent ones.

Haunting tale of the dustbowl

THE MOST ACCLAIMED novel of the year was John Steinbeck's *The Grapes of Wrath*. It tells the story of the Joad family, farmers in Oklahoma, whose land is blown away as dust in the great drought of the mid-thirties. They are forced to migrate westwards to California in search of work. The novel movingly tells of the ruthless way in which the dispossessed 'Okies' were treated as they desperately searched for a new livelihood in the America of the Depression years.

New faces in jazz

NEW NAMES IN JAZZ began to make their mark during 1939. Charlie Parker, the great master of the bebop saxophone, was first heard in New York during the year, whilst his opposite number on the trumpet, Dizzy Gillespie, was getting his first big break with Cab Calloway's house band at the famous Cotton Club. Meanwhile, T-Bone Walker and Charlie Christian were making the first ever recordings on the *electric* guitar – an instrument that was to have considerable impact on jazz and an even bigger effect on the emergence of rock and roll in the fifties. In a quieter vein, the pioneering jazz saxophonist Coleman Hawkins released his biggest ever hit 'Body and Soul' – which has remained part of jazz's repertoire of standards ever since. The Swing era might still be at its height, but signs of the future direction of jazz and popular music had begun to make themselves heard.

Nuclear project under way

IN JANUARY three German scientists, following the experiments carried out by the Italian physicist, Enrico Fermi, in 1934, worked on the splitting of uranium atoms. One of them, Lise Mietner, secretly left Germany and spread the news of their work. Gradually scientists in the outside world came to realize that Uranium 235 could be used to set off a chain reaction which would release enormous energy, an atomic bomb. The fear now was that Germany would develop a bomb before the rest of the world. These fears were deepened when in the summer, the German government banned the export of uranium from Czechoslovakia, a territory it now controlled.

The scientists enlisted the help of the most famous physicist of all, Albert Einstein. He quickly realized the importance of the developments. In October a letter signed by Einstein was delivered to President Roosevelt. It did the trick and Roosevelt ordered the secret development of further research under Enrico Fermi who was now living in America. So was born the Manhattan Project which led to the development of the first atomic bomb.

New water, air and land speed records

BY 1939 Sir Malcolm Campbell was concentrating on water speed records and on Coniston Water he set a new record of 141.74 miles per hour. Another Englishman, John Rhodes Cobb, challenged his land speed record reaching nearly 370 miles per hour at Utah. Meanwhile, a new air speed record of 484 miles per hour was set by a German, Fritz Wendel, in a Messershmidt.

Television closes down

ALL BRITISH television broadcasting was closed down for the period of the war. German bombers approaching Britain would have been able to pick up the signals and use them to guide their aircraft to their targets.

First transatlantic passenger service

PAN-AMERICAN AIRWAYS launched the first regular passenger service across the Atlantic on 20 June. The first flight covered 1900 miles in 13 hours 41 minutes. It carried 31 passengers and 787 kilograms of mail.

Blitzkrieg developed

AT THE END of the First World War tanks had only been able to travel at three miles per hour. By 1939 they could reach up to 30 miles per hour and thus could be used as a major weapon of attack. Aircraft had developed enormously too, both bombers and fighters. In fact, many experts believed that wars would be decided largely through the impact of bombing.

It was the Germans who made most use of the new technology. Combining the use of massed groups of tanks with raids by fighter planes, they developed blitzkrieg, 'lightning war'. It was the use of blitzkrieg which destroyed the Polish defences in September 1939.

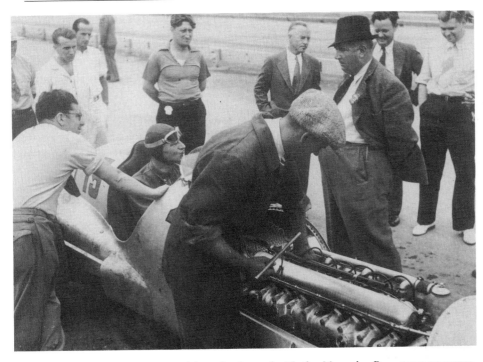

Dick Seaman, the British racing driver, is pictured with the Mercedes-Benz team manager, Neumeyer. Seaman started driving for the German Mercedes-Benz team in 1938 because of the lack of competitive British cars. He was killed in a crash in the 1939 Belgian Grand Prix. Adolf Hitler sent a wreath to Seaman's funeral.

Time Chart

World News	Sport and the Arts	Science and Technology

1930

(January) All farms in the Soviet Union declared collectives.
(March) Collectivization programme is relaxed after strong resistance of peasants.
(March–April) Gandhi's Salt March.
(April) London Naval Treaty signed.
(September) The Nazi Party wins 6,400,000 votes and 107 Reichstag seats in German elections.
(December) Unemployment in Britain reaches 2,500,000.

(March) D.H. Lawrence dies.
(April) The film *The Blue Angel* starring Marlene Dietrich is released.
(July) Uruguay wins football's first World Cup series.
Don Bradman sets a new test batting record of 334 runs.
(September) Bobby Jones completes the 'Grand Slam' by winning the US Amateur Golf Championship.

(February) Discovery of the planet Pluto.
(April) Amy Johnson completes her solo flight to Australia.
(October) Crash of R101 airship with loss of 44 lives.

1931

(April) Spain becomes a Republic.
(August) Formation of National Government in Britain.
Gandhi arrives in Britain for Round Table Conference on future of India.
(September) Britain goes off the Gold Standard, 25 other nations follow.
(October) Takeover of Manchuria by Japan.
(November) Statute of Westminster gives full independence to Dominions (including Australia, Canada and New Zealand).

(April) West Bromwich Albion win Cup Final beating Birmingham 2-1.
(October) Noel Coward's *Cavalcade* opens in London.
A large new record company, EMI, is formed after the merger of His Master's Voice and Columbia Records.

(February) Malcolm Campbell sets new land speed record of 245 m.p.h.
(May) Empire State Building is opened.
(September) George Stainforth sets a new air speed record of over 400 m.p.h.

1932

(February) Disarmament Conference opens.
Japanese announce Manchuria becomes the new 'independent' state of Manchukuo.
(July) Nazis become largest party in Germany after new elections.
(October) British Union of Fascists launched.
(November) Roosevelt wins US Presidential election.

(March) BBC begins its first broadcasts from the new Broadcasting House in London.
(July) Olympic Games are held in Los Angeles.
(November) The British writer John Galsworthy wins the Nobel Prize for Literature.

(April) Imperial Airways launch first regular service from London to Capetown.
(May) Amelia Earhart becomes the first woman to cross the Atlantic solo.
(December) George V makes the first Royal Christmas broadcast.

1933

(January) Hitler becomes Chancellor of Germany.
(February) Japan leaves League of Nations.
(March) Enabling law gives Nazis political control of Germany.
Roosevelt is inaugurated as President of the USA.
(October) Germany leaves the League of Nations.
(December) Unsuccessful Communist coup in Spain.

(January) Bodyline controversy rocks the cricket world.
(February) Bertolt Brecht, the playwright, leaves Germany in protest at Nazi rule. Many other artists and writers follow.
(March) Release of the film *King Kong*.
(September) Fred Perry becomes the first Briton to win the US Tennis Open for 30 years.

(March) Sir Malcolm Campbell sets new world landspeed record of 272 m.p.h.
(April) First flight over Mount Everest.
An Italian, Francesco Agello, becomes the fastest man in the air at 423 m.p.h.

1934

(January) Nazi Germany makes a ten year non-aggression pact with Poland.
(February) Major demonstrations in Paris lead to many deaths and injuries.
(June) The Night of Long Knives sees suppression of Hitler's enemies in Germany.
(July) Attempted Nazi take-over in Austria fails.
(August) Hitler takes on the title of Führer, or Leader, of Germany, following the death of President Hindenburg.
(September) The Soviet Union joins the League of Nations.
(October) Uprisings in Catalonia crushed by the Spanish government.
Long march begins in China.
(December) Assassination of Kirov in Leningrad.

(February) Death of the composer, Edward Elgar.
(June) Italy wins the World Cup in football.
(July) English players win both men's and women's singles titles at Wimbledon.

(July) The Mersey Tunnel, the world's longest underwater tunnel opened.
(September) The world's largest liner, the *Queen Mary*, launched on the River Clyde.

Time Chart

World News	Sport and the Arts	Science and Technology

1935

(March) Hitler announces rearmament of Germany. Italy, France and Britain protest without effect.
(June) Stanley Baldwin becomes British Prime Minister.
Anglo-German Naval Agreement.
Government of India Act passed.
(October) Italians invade Abyssinia.
The Long March ends in China.
(December) Hoare-Laval Pact on Abyssinia collapses after British government refuses to support it.

(May) US athlete, Jesse Owens, breaks five world records and equals a sixth in one day.
(August) Birth of Swing in the USA.

(September) Sir Malcolm Campbell becomes first man to exceed 300 m.p.h. on land.
(November) The new British Hurricane fighter makes its maiden flight.
(December) James Chadwick, the British physicist, is awarded a Nobel Prize for his work on neutrons.

1936

(February) Popular front parties win Spanish elections.
(March) Hitler marches into the Rhineland.
(May) Abyssinia falls and Mussolini proclaims the new Roman Empire.
(July) Army uprising in Spain leads to start of Spanish Civil War.
(August) The first show trials in the Soviet Union.
(November) Roosevelt elected President of the USA for second time.

(January) Death of Rudyard Kipling, the first British author to win the Nobel Prize.
(June) International Surrealist Exhibition in London arouses interest and controversy.
Berlin Olympics. Jesse Owens wins four gold medals.
(August) Poet and playwright Garcia Lorca dies, a casualty of the Spanish Civil War.

(February) The Volkswagen is launched in Germany.
(March) New British fighter plane, the Spitfire, makes its maiden flight.
(August) The BBC makes its first television broadcasts.

1937

(April) Bombing of the Basque town of Guernica by German air force.
(May) Neville Chamberlain becomes British Prime Minister.
(July) Peel Plan recommends division of Palestine.
(August) Japanese launch bombing raids on Chinese cities.
(September) Mussolini pays first visit to Hitler's Germany.
(November) Italy joins in an anti-Communist pact with Germany and Japan.

(January) Margot Fonteyn scores triumph in the role of 'Giselle' and is Britain's new prima ballerina.
(March) publication of George Orwell's *The Road to Wigan Pier*.
(June) Joe Louis wins world heavyweight boxing championship.

(April) Opening of world's longest suspension bridge, the Golden Gate in San Francisco.
(May) Crash of the airship *Hindenburg* in the USA.
BBC's first outside television broadcast (the Coronation of King George VI).
(October) Death of the physicist Ernest Rutherford.

1938

(March) Germany forms a Union (Anschluss) with Austria.
(April) Victories in the Spanish Civil War put Franco in dominating position over the Republicans.
(September) Munich Agreement allows Hitler to occupy western Czechoslovakia.
(November) 'Night of Broken Glass' in Germany.

(June) Italy wins the World Cup for the second time.
(July) Helen Moody wins Wimbledon finals for record eighth time.
(August) England scores a record 903 for 7 in Fifth Test Match.
(October) *War of the Worlds* radio play causes panic in the USA.

(January) First BBC foreign language broadcast (in Arabic).
(July) *Mallard* sets all time steam record of 126 m.p.h.
(August) *Queen Mary* sets new Atlantic crossing records both ways, beating its own records of 1936.
(September) Launching of the *Queen Elizabeth*, the world's largest passenger liner.

1939

(March) Capture of Madrid marks end of Spanish Civil War.
Occupation of remainder of Czechoslovakia by Germany.
(May) Pact of Steel between Hitler and Mussolini.
(August) Nazi-Soviet Pact.
(September) German invasion of Poland. Britain and France declare war on Germany.
Collapse of Poland.
(November) Soviet invasion of Finland.

(January) Death of W.B. Yeats.
(March) The Western *Stagecoach*, with John Wayne, released.
(August) Discovery of Sutton Hoo treasure.
The film *The Wizard of Oz* released.

(February) First nylon stockings go on sale in USA.
(June) Pan-American launches first regular passenger air service across the Atlantic.
(October) President Roosevelt approves research into the making of an atomic bomb.

Key figures of the decade

W.H. Auden (1907-1973)

THE ENGLISH POET who is remembered as one of the most important 'voices' of the 1930s, Auden expresses in his poems the anxieties of the age: the Depression; dictatorship and the coming of war. Auden visited Spain during the Civil War and, in one of his most famous poems, 'Spain', he explores the importance of the struggle to preserve freedom. By the time the Second World War came, however, Auden had gone to live in America, an escape which earned him much criticism.

Stanley Baldwin (1867-1947)

A BRITISH politician and leader of the Conservative Party from 1923 to 1937, Baldwin became Prime Minister, as leader of the National Government, for the third time in 1935. He presented himself as a calm and steady leader who would bring stability to Britain after the years of the Depression. It was his refusal to accept Mrs Simpson as Queen which led to the abdication of King Edward VIII in 1936. While popular at home, Baldwin did little to prepare Britain to face the threats posed by Germany. He retired in 1937.

Busby Berkeley (1895-1976)

THE AMERICAN film director and choreographer was famous for his spectacular dancing girl extravaganzas of the early 1930s such as *Gold Diggers of 1933* and *Footlight Parade*. Rich costumes and cleverly filmed chorus lines made his films an escape from the realities of the Depression.

Neville Chamberlain (1869-1940)

A BRITISH politician and Chancellor of the Exchequer from 1931 to 1937, Chamberlain succeeded Stanley Baldwin as Prime Minister and leader of the Conservative Party in 1937. He is chiefly remembered for his attempts to keep peace with Germany through the policy of appeasement, which involved negotiations and concessions over areas of dispute. The policy failed, and Chamberlain led Britain into war in September 1939 when Hitler invaded Poland. He resigned as Prime Minister in 1940 and died shortly afterwards.

Chiang Kaishek (1887-1975)

ORIGINALLY A SOLDIER, Chiang came to power in China in 1928 as the head of a nationalist government. He reunified the country after years of chaos but immediately faced opposition from both Communists and, more seriously in the 1930s, the Japanese. Unable to prevent the Japanese conquest of Manchuria and much of Northern China, he had retreated with his armies to central China by the end of the decade. He was later overthrown by Mao Zedong.

Albert Einstein (1879-1955)

EINSTEIN WAS A GERMAN nuclear physicist and already an internationally known figure by the 1930s for his theory of relativity. He left Germany for the USA in 1933 and campaigned against the threat of war that he believed Hitler posed. In 1939 Einstein, learning of the possible development of an atomic bomb by German scientists, persuaded President Roosevelt to start American research into such a bomb.

Francisco Franco (1892-1975)

AFTER A BRILLIANT early career as a Spanish army officer, Franco became one of the leaders of the army revolt against the Republican government in 1936 which began the Spanish Civil War. In October of that year he was declared leader of the Nationalists. He co-ordinated his followers more successfully than the Republicans and led them to victory in 1939, remaining dictator of Spain for the rest of his life.

Mahatma Gandhi (1869-1948)

ORIGINALLY A LAWYER, Gandhi spent many years fighting racial discrimination in South Africa before returning to his native India to become one of the leaders of the nationalist Congress Party there. His campaigns against the British were strictly non-violent but he was still imprisoned on several occasions during the decade. Gandhi also campaigned against oppression within Indian society.

Greta Garbo (1905-1990)

A SWEDISH ACTRESS, Garbo was one of the few stars of the silent films of the 1920s to transfer successfully to the talkies. In films such as *Grand Hotel* (1932), *Queen Christina* (1933) and *Anna Karenina* (1935) her beauty and

Key figures of the decade

astonishing screen power made her a legend.

Adolf Hitler (1889-1945)

ADOLF HITLER came to power in Germany in 1933, after ruthlessly exploiting the anxieties and humiliations felt by many Germans after their defeat in the First World War and during the Depression. Once in power, Hitler consolidated his control with increasing brutality, particularly against the Jews who were seen as a major threat to the German people. Hitler also rearmed Germany and prepared for a war of conquest to the east. He took over Austria in 1938 and Czechoslovakia in 1938 and 1939. It was his attack on Poland in September 1939 which unleashed the Second World War.

Amy Johnson (1903-1941)

JOHNSON WAS AN ENGLISH aviator who embarked on a solo flight from England to Australia in 1930, never having flown a journey of more than 200 miles before. Her flight captured the imagination of the world. She completed several record-breaking flights, including one over Siberia and the fastest solo flight between Capetown and London. She was lost during a flight over Britain in 1941.

Mao Zedong (1893-1976)

A FOUNDER MEMBER of the Chinese Communist Party (1921), Mao faced increasing pressure from the Chinese Nationalist government in the 1930s.

He led his communist followers on the Long March across China until they found safety in a remote area of the north. In 1936 Mao, now firmly leader of the Communists, agreed to fight with the Nationalists against the Japanese invaders.

Benito Mussolini (1883-1945)

MUSSOLINI came to power as dictator of Italy in 1922 and attempted to transform his country into a Fascist state on the principles of authority, national pride and the glorification of war. In 1935, to increase support for his regime, he invaded the African country of Abyssinia, conquering it by 1936 and proclaiming a new 'Roman Empire'. In the late 1930s he drew increasingly close to Hitler's Germany, signing an alliance with Hitler in 1939 and joining the Second World War on Germany's side in 1940.

George Orwell (1903-1950)

BORN IN INDIA and educated in England, Orwell first became a policeman in Burma. He hated the British Empire, however, and was back in England by the 1930s struggling to become a writer. A socialist, he went to Spain in 1937 to fight for the Republicans. He established his reputation with novels published in the 1930s and his documentary *The Road to Wigan Pier* (1937), but became famous with his later works *1984* and *Animal Farm*.

Jesse Owens (1913-1980)

OWENS WAS A black American athlete who dominated the sport in the mid-1930s. In only one day in 1935 he broke five world records and equalled another. His world long jump record was not equalled for 25 years. In 1936 Owens was one of the American team at the Berlin Olympics. His four gold medals there came as a massive blow for the Nazi organizers who claimed that blacks were inferior in every way to whites.

Franklin Roosevelt (1882-1945)

US President from 1932 to 1945, Roosevelt was the only President in history to have been elected three times. He is remembered for bringing a new air of optimism to an America overwhelmed by the Depression. His so-called 'New Deal' helped the US economy to revive. Although the USA cut itself off from the rest of the world in this decade, Roosevelt was one of the first to see that his country could not stand aside from the Second World War.

Josef Stalin (1879-1953)

STALIN BECAME LEADER of the Soviet Union in the 1920s. During the 1930s he transformed the nation into an industrial state though at enormous cost. Infamous for his massive purges, he obliterated all suspected enemies. In 1939 he signed a non-aggression pact with Hitler which brought him two years of peace before the Germans invaded the Soviet Union in 1941.

Books for further reading

Books about the 1930s:

Hugh Brogan, *Longman History of the United States of America*, Longman, 1985

Harry Browne, *Spain's Civil War*, Longman, 1983

Peter Calvocoressi and Guy Wint, *Total War: Causes and Courses of the Second World War*, Penguin, 1974

John Carey, *The Faber Book of Reportage*, Faber, 1987

Harrison Evans Salisbury, *The Long March*, Pan Books, 1986

Tony Howarth, *20th Century History: The World since 1900*, Longman, 1987

Gabriel Jackson, *A Concise History of the Spanish Civil War*, Thames and Hudson, 1980

Martin McCauley, *Stalin and Stalinism*, Longman, 1983

Denis Mack Smith, *Mussolini*, Paladin Books, 1983

R. McNeal, *Stalin, Man and Ruler*, Oxford University Press.

William Manchester, *The Glory and the Dream*, Michael Joseph, 1975

Norman Stone, *Hitler, An Introduction*, Coronet Books, 1982

D.G. Williamson, *The Third Reich*, Longman, 1982

Social History:

Christabel Bielenberg, *The Past is Myself*, Corgi, 1984

David A. Cook, *A History of Narrative Film*, W.W. Norton, 1982

Charles Freeman, *Britain in the 1930s*, Batsford, 1985

Richard Grunberger, *A Social History of the Third Reich*, Penguin, 1974

Nadezhda Mandelstam *Hope Against Hope*, Harvill Press, 1961

George Orwell, *The Road to Wigan Pier*, 1937

John Stevenson, *British Society 1914-45*, Penguin, 1984

Some novels of the 1930s:

Walter Greenwood, *Love on the Dole*

Ernest Hemingway, *For Whom the Bell Tolls*

George Orwell, *Keep the Aspidistra Flying, Coming Up for Air*

John Steinbeck, *The Grapes of Wrath*

Acknowledgments

The Author and Publishers would like to thank the following for permission to reproduce illustrations: the Batsford Archives for pages 4 (bottom), 21, 23, 25, 44 and 65; the Beamish North of England Open Air Museum for the frontispiece; the Bridgeman Art Library for page 52; the Electricity Council for page 35; the Hulton-Deutsch Collection for the cover (bottom right) and pages 4 (top), 11, 13, 18, 28, 33, 37, 48 and 60; the Imperial War Museum for pages 24, 30, 31, 54 and 62; the National Portrait Gallery for page 39; the National Railway Museum for page 59; Popperfoto for the front and back covers and pages 3, 5, 6, 7, 8, 10, 14, 15, 16, 19, 20, 26, 34, 36, 38, 40, 41, 42, 43, 45, 46, 47, 49, 51, 53, 55, 56, 57 and 63; RCHME for page 22. The illustration on page 17 was drawn by Nance Lui Fyson who also researched the pictures.

Index

Numbers in **bold** type refer to illustrations

Index